MW01518226

Stigma, Storytelling, and Adolescent Parents' Children

Stigma, Storytelling, and Adolescent Parents' Children

Nothing to Prove

Eryn N. Bostwick and Amy Janan Johnson

LEXINGTON BOOKS

Lanham • Boulder • New York • London

Published by Lexington Books
An imprint of The Rowman & Littlefield Publishing Group, Inc.
4501 Forbes Boulevard, Suite 200, Lanham, Maryland 20706
www.rowman.com

86-90 Paul Street, London EC2A 4NE

British Library Cataloguing in Publication Information Available

Library of Congress Cataloging-in-Publication Data

Names: Bostwick, Eryn N., author. | Johnson, Amy Janan, author.
Title: Stigma, storytelling, and adolescent parents' children: nothing to prove / Eryn N. Bostwick and Amy Janan Johnson.
Description: Lanham : Lexington Books, [2023] | Includes bibliographical references and index.
Identifiers: LCCN 2022052149 (print) | LCCN 2022052150 (ebook) | ISBN 9781793638113 (cloth) | ISBN 9781793638120 (ebook)
Subjects: LCSH: Teenage parents—Social conditions. | Children of teenage mothers—Social conditions. | Children of teenage mothers—Psychology. | Stigma (Social psychology)
Classification: LCC HQ759.64 .B67 2023 (print) | LCC HQ759.64 (ebook) | DDC 306.874/3—dc23/eng/20221122
LC record available at https://lccn.loc.gov/2022052149
LC ebook record available at https://lccn.loc.gov/2022052150

♾™ The paper used in this publication meets the minimum requirements of American National Standard for Information Sciences—Permanence of Paper for Printed Library Materials, ANSI/NISO Z39.48-1992.

Dedication
This book is dedicated to Eryn's parents and to all of those born to adolescent parents who struggle with the burden no one ever said they had to carry. Always remember, you are enough.

Contents

Acknowledgments

Eryn N. Bostwick

As this book is based on the results of Eryn's dissertation research, she would like to start by thanking her advisor and coauthor, Dr. Amy Janan Johnson, and her committee members: Dr. Ann Beutel, Dr. Ryan Bisel, Dr. Ioana Cionea, and Dr. Norman Wong for their guidance throughout the dissertation process. It was a long and tedious ride, but you all helped her navigate any issues that arose and kept her on track. She'd also like to thank her fellow graduate students, her friends who have become family, for always being available for random text and phone conversations to work through her concerns and for reminding her that the best dissertation is a done dissertation. Thank you to Eryn's coworkers at Cleveland State for supporting her during the year and a half when she both taught full-time and worked on her dissertation. Their support and guidance were invaluable. Thank you to the study participants for taking time out of their days to help Eryn achieve her dreams. Thank you to Eryn's family for always listening with open hearts and open minds as she rambled on and on about what she was working on. Thank you to Eryn's in-laws for opening their home to her for one of the most difficult years of her PhD program. Thank you to her parents for always supporting her in anything she does, and particularly for supporting this project. Lastly, thank you to Eryn's husband for holding the pieces of their life together while she focused so extensively on her work. There were days she did not know how she was going to finish while also maintaining all of her work-and-life-related responsibilities (and many days she did not), but he always kept her going. Thank you for his patience, for his love, and for his support.

Amy Janan Johnson

Amy wishes to thank her family, friends, and colleagues who have given her the inspiration to continue to pursue a career as a mentor, teacher, and research scholar for over 20 years. Many thanks to Dr. Eryn Bostwick as well for allowing her to be a part of this important project.

.

Introduction

"I am enough." This statement, though simple, is one too many people do not believe. A quick Google search shows books with this statement as their title, and jewelry with the phrase that people can purchase. In fact, the first author of this book has a bracelet with the phrase imprinted on it that she wears every day, as well as a plaque with the phrase sitting prominently in her living room. Why does this phrase seem to resonate with so many? Because, unfortunately, oftentimes the messages people receive throughout their lives convince them the opposite is true: that they are not enough. That they must prove their worth to others. That they can earn being "enough" through doing, by constantly trying to do enough to show they are, in fact, worthy. One problem with this type of thinking is that it is nearly impossible to achieve worthiness in this way. There is never a time when someone can say they have finally done enough to prove their worth. The process is exhausting and demoralizing.

This phrase "I am enough," and the ways in which seeking to prove oneself influence one's behaviors and self-esteem, inspired the work of this book. This book utilizes previous scholarship and the results of a study conducted by the authors to highlight how various messages influence the identity of those born to adolescent parents. In what follows, this introduction lays out the basic argument of the authors—that one's identity is influenced by both societal and interpersonal messages heard throughout one's life and that negative messages related to one's identity influence how people interpret their life experiences. This introduction also delineates why this book is focused on the population of those born to adolescent parents when, admittedly, many types of people can relate to the experience of feeling unworthy. Lastly, this introduction outlines some basic information about the original research study described in this book. The authors hope the information presented here, and throughout the rest of the book, resonates and helps people realize that they are, in fact, enough.

WHAT IS IDENTITY?

Generally speaking, when people talk about their identity, they are referring to their perception of who they are as individuals. The research focused on better understanding identity has examined how one's identity is established, different factors that might influence the identity formation process, and life outcomes associated with identity-related factors and issues (Koenig Kellas 2005; McAdams 1993; Mead 1934). For example, one of the commonly explored identity-related factors is self-esteem, which refers to an individual's subjective evaluation of their social standing. Self-esteem can have either a positive or negative influence on a person's overall identity (Kranstuber and Koenig Kellas 2011).

From a scholarly perspective, identity is a multifaceted concept, and researchers generally believe one's identity is influenced by the messages people receive about themselves throughout their lives (Mead 1934). For example, if someone tells another person they are smart and capable, that person may begin considering "smart" and "capable" to be characteristics of themselves. This process of forming one's identity never really ends, although as one gets older, people may feel more confident in who they are and therefore be less likely to willingly accept the messages of others.

Many people experience a life crisis at some point often asking themselves such common but profound questions such as Who am I? What am I doing here? What is my purpose? Sometimes this crisis results in thoughts of worthlessness, or someone feeling like they are not enough, often leading them to question how they got to this point.

Understanding how the messages one has received throughout their life have had an influence on one's identity can be eye-opening and therapeutic. Research by scholars such as Mead (1934) and McAdams (1993) suggests if someone wants to understand how they developed their personal identity, they should consider the types of messages they have heard throughout their life. This assessment can be a daunting process because people hear so many messages, how can anyone ever keep track or remember them all? Oftentimes, many people might not even realize how influential certain messages have been throughout their lives, but this fact is exactly why it is important to stop and reflect on even the most seemingly innocuous interactions from one's past.

According to Mead (1932), there are two main types of messages that influence the development of one's identity. The first is *societal* messages and the second is *interpersonal* messages. Societal messages refer to the ways one's overall culture and/or society talks about certain groups of people. Sometimes society sends direct messages about one's identity, for example, perhaps when influential politicians or leaders make public statements about whether some aspect of one's identity is "acceptable." Consider, how a woman struggling with infertility might feel if a well-known politician gives a speech suggesting that biological motherhood is the pinnacle of a woman's life experience. She may struggle with the question: Does her life mean less because she is not a biological mother?

Other times the messages one hears from society are indirect and are reflected in the ways people talk about what is "normal" and what is "abnormal." Additionally, the policies the society in question upholds as ethical might indirectly suggest who is acceptable and who is not (Mead 1932). For example, how might legislation that is against adoption for same-sex couples and related policies influence how people define a "family" in the United States? If policies say that same-sex partners cannot adopt, and people from that society consider children an essential requirement for being a family, are same-sex partners not able to be "real" families?

If one's family experience is typical and matches what society would consider the "norm" to be, then they may never consider these types of questions. Instead, it is those that exist in the margins, those that differ in some way from what people expect, who are more likely to feel like society has called them out for being different. Their "otherness" is highlighted for them by society; it becomes an aspect of their identity that is hard to escape because society seems to be constantly pointing it out. This "otherness" often leads to the need to manage the identity of one's family and legitimize one's own family form as "real" and "good." Family communication scholar Kathleen Galvin (2006) developed a term, *discourse-dependent* families, that relates to this experience. Galvin says all families must utilize discourse, in the form of communication, to define their family composition to both family insiders and outsiders. Rather than relying on biological or legal ties to define what a family is, scholars taking a discourse-dependent approach to understanding families consider families to be groups of people that share intimate bonds and group identity (Fitzpatrick and Vangelisti 1995). Communication is central to this experience because it is through communication that people develop close bonds and form/manage group identity.

This bond-building and identity-forming communication behavior occur both within the family system among family members and with outsiders (Galvin 2006). For example, within the family, members may tell one another stories that bring them closer together as a unit, while outside the family, members may engage in a defense of their family form to outsiders who seek to attack it (i.e., children of single parents defending their family form to others). While all families are technically discourse-dependent, family communication scholars often utilize the term "discourse-dependent families" to refer to those that must engage in this type of communication (both within and outside of the family) more frequently than others. For example, families whose structure differs from what society considers a "true" family would likely need to defend their family to outsiders more often than those whose family appears to match the societal definition. In America, historically this societal definition means that any family that does not match the definition of the nuclear family, a family with two heterosexual married parents that have biological children after marriage, could be labeled a discourse-dependent family. This topic will be explored in more depth in later chapters.

Societal Messages, Interpersonal Messages, and Identity

Various scholars have examined the role that societal messages play in "othering" people for decades. Perhaps the most famous is Erving Goffman's research on stigma and stigmatization. According to Goffman (1963), *stigma* refers to a label associated with a characteristic or attribute others perceive as negative or harmful. Because people tend to fear others that are different, it is common for those who grow up with something other than the nuclear family form to receive a stigmatized label (Galvin 2006).

If stigma is the specific label, *stigmatization* is the process whereby people with the negative label are treated differently by others. In essence, stigmatization represents one way societal messages of people's "otherness" are communicated to themselves and others. It is one's experience with stigmatization that alerts them to the fact that they are different and not in a positive way.

However, messages from society are not the only type of message that influence people's lives and identities. Mead (1932) notes that interpersonal messages, or the messages people hear from certain individuals throughout their lives, are also influential. For example, if someone was constantly told that they were an "old soul" when they were younger, they might adopt that characteristic and start to think about themselves as an "old soul." Two examples of interpersonal messages that researchers have highlighted as important to personal identity development are family stories and memorable messages (Koenig Kellas and Kranstuber Horstman 2015). *Family stories* are a specific type of story that reflect what family members find significant in their lives and the life of the family as a whole (Stone 1988). *Memorable messages* refer to verbal messages people remember, hear relatively early in life, and consider influential in some way (Knapp, Stohl, and Reardon 1981).

The interpersonal messages people hear are important because they provide an opportunity to either confirm or reject the messages society sends to them. For example, think about someone who struggles with their mental health. Society might tell them that there is something wrong with them and they should be ashamed, but their family and friends may reject that societal message and tell stories highlighting the idea that there is nothing shameful about struggling with one's mental health. If the individual in question takes the messages from family and friends to heart, they may be more able to ignore the negative societal messages, ultimately avoiding stigmatizing themselves or accepting these negative societal messages into their identity.

The preceding examples illustrate how influential both societal and interpersonal messages can be to one's identity. Another important factor, which became clear as the authors analyzed the data collected from those born to adolescent parents for this book, is how the internalization of societal and interpersonal messages influences how people interpret the experiences around them. A later chapter in this book details how stories about some adverse outcomes associated with adolescent pregnancy coupled with messages from one's family about how hard being an adolescent parent is can lead children of adolescent parents to feel guilty about their parents' experiences and ultimately feel like they must prove any struggle their parents went through was worth it that, in essence, their existence was worth their parents' struggles.

WHY THOSE BORN TO ADOLESCENT PARENTS?

The goal of this book is to explore the ways in which societal messages and interpersonal messages have influenced the identity formation of those born to adolescent parents. If societal and interpersonal messages influence the identity development of everyone, as Mead (1932) suggests, then why does this book focus specifically on those born to adolescent parents? What unique aspects of identity formation may be specifically relevant to them?

One reason for the choice of this specific population is because the authors wanted to examine a family type in which family members have likely heard many potentially negative societal messages over their lifetime. Although circumstances have changed since the peak of societal concerns about adolescent parenting in the 1980s and 1990s, there are still strong anti-adolescent parenting societal messages in the United States. Additionally, just because societal messages were sent decades ago does not mean they do not matter currently. For example, between the 1960s and 1990s, it was common for politicians and others in societal positions of power to refer to adolescent pregnancy as an "epidemic" and something that led to the demise of the traditional family (Furstenberg 2007). Those who were born and/or grew up within that 40-year time period could still be dealing with the fallout from those messages, even if they are no longer as widely broadcast publicly.

Second, examining how adolescent parents navigate the negative views concerning adolescent parenthood provides a great context to explore how people can use interpersonal messages to mitigate harm to one's identity caused by societal messages, particularly stories those born to adolescent parents hear focused on their concept, birth, or existence. For example, one of the common messages people hear about adolescent parenthood is that the adolescent parent is destined for failure because they had a child so young. Parents who talk to their children about how hard their life is because they were a young parent might inadvertently repeat and reinforce this negative societal message, increasing chances their children will conclude that their existence made their parents' lives harder, resulting in a more negative self-identity. Alternatively, those parents who talk about how much their children have added to their lives might help their children avoid adopting the negative societal messaging as part of their identity.

Third, there are characteristics of families of adolescent parents that align with the definition of "discourse-dependent." For example, families of adolescent parents do not follow the typical social script for family development, thus highlighting them as different from the very beginning of family formation. Instead of meeting, getting married, and then having children, not only do many (but not all) members of these families engage in a different timeline in which children come before marriage, but they also become parents while still technically children themselves. This deviation could result in the family's need to explain their timeline and how it came to be to others and themselves. Additionally, aspects of the family structure itself could make these families discourse-dependent. For example, if adolescent parents have other children later in life, meaning they have children many years apart (one or more as adolescents and other children when they are adults), people who are actually siblings may appear as parent-child dyads to outsiders. Therefore, when they are out in public, members of these families might have to explain their sibling relationship to others.

The final reason for the focus on adolescent parenthood is that the first author, Eryn, was born to adolescent parents, and throughout her life has constantly struggled with her identity. When she learned about the influences societal and interpersonal messages can have on how one defines themself, she started reflecting on the family stories she had been told growing up and how those stories may have intermingled with messages from society to influence how she felt about herself as a child of adolescent parents. She realized that if she saw connections, she likely was not the only one to feel this way, so she set off to talk to other people born to adolescent parents to learn more about their own personal experiences and to consider how these experiences can inform the process of identity formation for other children of adolescent parents.

The Study and Resulting Data

The data presented in this book are based on the first author's dissertation research, which involved collecting survey data from 141 people who were over the age of 18 at the time of data collection and born to adolescent parents. The first author asked about their experiences growing up, the societal messages they and their families received about their parents' status as an adolescent parent, the stories they heard about their birth/existence growing up, and their self-esteem, which was used as a proxy to measure identity.

Prior to collecting data for this study, the authors ran a pilot study utilizing college students at a large southwestern university. This allowed them to (1) test survey flow, (2) make sure the survey was not too long, thus resulting in high numbers of attrition, and most importantly, (3) ensure the survey items were reliable and valid prior to conducting the main analysis.

After the pilot study was completed, collecting data for the main study took many months, as finding people born to adolescent parents was not easy, but after posting the study on multiple social media outlets, reaching out to multiple professional organizations and adolescent parenting discussion boards, asking students at multiple universities to participate if they met the criteria, and utilizing Amazon's MTurk worker program, the authors finally had 141 usable responses.

After collecting survey data, the first author then interviewed eight of the survey participants in great depth to learn more about their experiences with societal and interpersonal messages surrounding their status as a person born to an adolescent parent. Interviews focused specifically on learning more about (1) the most stigmatizing experiences interviewees noted going through in their surveys, (2) the most influential stories focused on their conception, birth, and/or existence they remembered hearing while growing (again, as identified in their survey responses), and (3) how their understanding of their experiences with stigma and the stories they were told has changed over time. Details about how and why these specific people were chosen to participate in the interview are provided in Appendix A found at the end of this book. Interview results reported in this book utilize pseudonyms in order to protect the identity of research participants.

More details about data collection and methodological and analytical decisions can be found in Appendix B: Descriptive Data About Research Participants and Appendix A: Methodology at the end of the book. Additionally, survey questions Eryn used and the questions asked during the interviews can be found in Appendix C: Survey Questions and Appendix D: Interview Schedule, respectively, for those interested in learning more about the specific procedures. Also, readers are invited to email the first author at e.bostwick@

tcu.edu if they would like more information about either the methods used to collect data and/or the analytical decisions made by the authors.

WHAT TO EXPECT

Chapter 1 begins by discussing views of adolescent parenthood in America. This discussion is important because it helps to outline various societal messages associated with adolescent parenthood and how those messages might encourage stigmatization of adolescent parents and their family members. The second chapter explores the influence of *interpersonal* messages from family members regarding adolescent parenthood on those born to adolescent parents, with a specific focus on how family stories either support or challenge messages from society. Chapter 3 delineates how the combination of societal and interpersonal messages can sometimes lead to a sense of being a "burden" for those born to adolescent parents, while chapter 4 talks about how to overcome the belief that one is a burden. Finally, chapter 5 gives some suggestions for what people can do to help those born to adolescent parents develop a positive view of themselves. Relevant results from the survey and interviews will be integrated throughout all the chapters to show how this research can help inform and expand people's understanding of identity formation among children of adolescent parents.

Chapter 1

Perceptions of Adolescent Parenthood in the United States and the Influence of Stigmatization

PERCEPTIONS IN SOCIETY

Given Mead's (1934) assertion that societal messaging influences people's identity, one must first seek to understand how the experiences of those born to adolescent parents relate to the larger national social and cultural context of the United States. So, what is the current overall perception of adolescent parenthood in the United States? For a long time adolescent parenthood was considered a public health and social problem and not just any problem but as health crisis. In fact, over the years adolescent pregnancy has been described as an epidemic (Furstenberg 2007). The term "epidemic" is defined by Merriam-Webster as something characterized by widespread growth throughout a community and is often tied to the term "disease." By calling adolescent pregnancy an epidemic, society highlighted the belief that adolescent pregnancy is something that spreads and harms people, something that needs to be controlled and stopped.

Certainly, equating adolescent pregnancy with a disease helps to send a negative message about adolescent parents to the parents themselves and others. If adolescent pregnancy is a disease, then the parents themselves are diseased. And if adolescent parents are diseased because they became pregnant at a young age, what does that make the child? Are they, in fact, the disease, and how might that label influence how they view themselves? Even if those born to adolescent parents do not think of themselves as "diseased" per say, there are plenty of other societal messages about adolescent parenthood that paint these families in a negative light. For example, common societal beliefs about adolescent parenthood include the assumption that such parenthood is always a mistake or that those born to adolescent parents are destined for failure.

Why would negative messaging about adolescent parenthood classifying it as a *disease* matter? Because these words influence how people view and treat others, even subconsciously, and such treatment can have long-term consequences. For example, when responding to a survey question asking about children of adolescent parents' most influential experience being treated poorly because of their parents' age, multiple participants reported being told that they were a mistake, something that can easily weigh on a person and encourage them to question their worth. Another common message participants identified was the idea that they were destined to "fail" in some way, whether that be related to performing poorly in school, engaging in delinquent behaviors, or becoming adolescent parents themselves. For example, one study participant wrote,

> I had a parent-teacher conference. Nothing bad just to update my mom on how I was doing and to answer any questions my mom might have. Well, I went into the class with my mom and the teacher said. "Oh, that's your mom." I said yes. She said, "Oh I'm really surprised you have such good grades." I was confused. But after the conference the next day my teacher said, "I hope your grades don't drop and you stop going to school." I asked her why would she say that. Her exact words: "Because your mom is so young it is going to happen. I've seen it so many times." She treated me differently the whole school year. (37-year-old participant whose mother was 16 and father was 18 when they were born)

The fact that those born to adolescent parents remember these messages and self-identify them as having a lasting negative influence on their lives shows how harmful societal messages can be.

It is important to consider that societal messaging does not exist in a vacuum; the messages society sends about adolescent parenthood are related to the broader historical and political context in the United States. In fact, societal beliefs about adolescent parenthood have even influenced political platforms and legislation. Even if adolescent parents and/or those born to adolescent parents do not receive direct messages from people reflecting negative societal beliefs, like the participant quoted previously, hearing your family form described negatively as part of a political debate or political legislation can be hurtful. Therefore, the next section explains the historical and political context related to negative societal messages about adolescent parenthood.

Historical and Political Context

Researcher Frank Furstenberg (2007) examined societal messages about adolescent pregnancy and claims such messages became prominent shortly after the sexual revolution of the 1960s, when rates of adolescent pregnancy were actually at their peak. Interestingly, he found the public became more obsessed with the idea of controlling rates of adolescent pregnancy in the late 1960s and 1970s, by which time the *actual* rates of adolescent pregnancy had decreased. Worries about the adolescent pregnancy "epidemic" picked up again in the 1990s after then-president Bill Clinton identified it as the country's most serious social problem in a 1995 address (Furstenberg 2007). However, at the time of Clinton's address, the rate of adolescent pregnancy was just over half of what it had been at the 1960s peak. Despite statistical improvement, by labeling adolescent pregnancy as a social problem, and a pressing one at that, people became obsessed with finding ways to eradicate it.

To stop the spread of this "disease," politicians enacted policies and developed programs aimed to control and minimize instances of adolescent pregnancy. For example, a federal welfare law passed in 1996 contained provisions meant to reduce or eliminate instances of adolescent pregnancy. These provisions included $50 million to invest in abstinence education, a requirement that states take steps to reduce out-of-wedlock pregnancies with a focus on adolescent pregnancy specifically and the ability for states to deny adolescent parents their welfare benefits if they have more than one child while on welfare (Furstenberg 2007). The problem was perceived as so large, as so important, that the government invested money in eradicating it, and the message to adolescent parents was clear: you are a problem and if you cannot control yourself, you will be punished. Unfortunately, adolescent parents and their children have reported that messages focusing on the "problem" of adolescent parenthood have been extremely detrimental to them (Barcelos and Gubrium 2014), but why does this occur?

How Do Societal Beliefs About Adolescent Parenthood Influence the Treatment of Adolescent Parents?

One way negative societal beliefs about adolescent parenthood filter down to influence interpersonal interactions is via the media. Kelly (1996) examined the ways in which the media in the 1980s and 1990s talked about adolescent parents and uncovered four different types of commentary, or *frames*, that she argued reflected the cultural and societal discourse surrounding adolescent parenthood. The first frame was the *bureaucratic expert frame*, which focuses on psychological reasons why pregnant adolescents want to keep their babies. According to Kelly, the focus on why an adolescent would choose to keep a child places the "problem" of adolescent pregnancy within the individual and ignores the larger societal context that might influence the likelihood that someone becomes an adolescent parent, such as poverty. Furthermore, this specific frame assumes the pregnancy was a mistake, which would suggest the child was unplanned and perhaps even unwanted.

The second frame was the *wrong family frame*, which involves concern over what adolescent parenting means to the fate of the traditional family structure. The *wrong family frame* suggests adolescent mothers are bad, especially because this frame assumes adolescent parents rely on government programs for economic resources (consider the welfare reform bill in 1996 for evidence as to how prominent this view became).

The third frame was the *wrong society frame*, which focuses on highlighting outside factors that lead to adolescent pregnancy, instead of blaming adolescent parents for their circumstances. The *wrong society frame* aims to reduce negative perceptions of individuals associated with adolescent pregnancy; however, Kelly (1996) found mainstream media very rarely utilized this frame.

Lastly, the fourth frame was the *stigma is wrong frame*, which was usually depicted by the personal views of adolescent mothers' themselves. This frame suggests the mother's choice, no matter what their choice is (adoption, keeping the baby, etc.), should be respected and not thought of as wrong or negative.

The media frames that Kelly (1996) identified are important because such media portrayals can subconsciously affect how people view and treat others. For example, in the 2009 book *Breaking the Adolescent Parent Cycle*, Westman suggests the state should remove children from their mothers if the mother is under the age of 18 because it is safe to assume she is neglectful. This portrayal directly relates to the *wrong family frame* identified by Kelly, and importantly, even though Kelly identified the *wrong family frame* based on media coverage in the 1990s, Westman was repeating this messaging as late as 2009. Obviously, painting adolescent parents with these broad brushstrokes is not accurate and suggestions like Westman's send harmful messages about the ability of adolescent parents to take care of their children, as well as their value to society.

Unfortunately, negative beliefs about adolescent parenthood are not limited to books like Westman's, and messages like his can also influence how complete strangers treat those born to adolescent parents. For example, when opening up about a particularly hurtful situation, one survey participant wrote,

> I have been judged many times as a child of teenage parents but the worst I can remember was a time when a lady told my mom she should have given me up for adoption to have a better life. No teenage mom can properly care for a child, she told her. (46-year-old participant whose mother was 18 and father was 19 when they were born)

Perhaps particularly troubling is the way in which negative societal beliefs about adolescent parenthood influence how those principally tasked with helping and supporting members of adolescent parents treat them as well, such as healthcare workers. Therefore, the following section talks about treatment of adolescent parents and their children in healthcare settings.

Negative Treatment in Healthcare Settings

According to Brand, Morrison, and Down (2014), healthcare providers often focus on the moral and social responsibilities of adolescent parents. Brand et al. argue that such a focus feeds into a "blaming the victim" mentality, which then extends to how the wider community views adolescent parents, and ultimately has a strong influence on how adolescents experience parenthood. In fact, their research highlighted that adolescent parents believe their lives are constantly under a spotlight and that they are continually under surveillance by the public. These parents were able to directly relate the fear of surveillance to public messaging suggesting young mothers are dependent upon welfare (Brand, Morrison, and Down 2014). Brand et al. suggest this fear also deteriorates trust between young parents and care providers, which leads to young parents avoiding care because they fear their parental capabilities will be judged.

Given the wide implications of negative treatment in healthcare settings, particularly its role in perpetuating the "blaming the victim" mentality, one must wonder how this treatment filters down to influence the children of adolescent parents. Responses from interview participants provide some insight. For example, Manuel,[1] a 35-year-old Hispanic male whose parents were both 17 when he was born, explained that he constantly felt responsible for his parents' economic struggles, a circumstance directly related to negative societal messages about adolescent parents' inevitable failure.

The evidence provided thus far shows that societal messages surrounding adolescent pregnancy have been negative in tone, particularly in the 1990s when political conversations surrounding the "epidemic" of adolescent pregnancy were at their peak. It also shows that these messages filtered down to influence how adolescent parents and those born to adolescent parents have been treated by others, such as healthcare workers. At this point it is also important to note that although the peak of negative messaging occurred in the 1990s, this fact does not mean the ramifications of those messages no longer matter or are not relevant. Westman's 2009 book clearly illustrates that these messages live on. Additionally, as those born in the late 1980s and 1990s grew up surrounded by these negative messages, it is likely the influences the messages have had on them still linger. To understand how and why negative messages can remain so influential over time, examining processes surrounding stigma and stigmatization is helpful.

The Connection Between Societal Perceptions and Stigmatization

To understand how and why societal views influence adolescent parents and their children, one first must understand how stigma relates to the process of stigmatization. Goffman's (1963) definition of stigma refers to a label associated with a characteristic or attribute others find negative or harmful. Pescosolido and Martin (2015) have identified four criteria that a characteristic must meet to be considered stigmatized. First, the characteristic must be associated with *distinguishing and labeling*, meaning others must delineate someone with the characteristic as different from themselves and place them into a category because of this distinctiveness. Second, the differences in question must be associated with *negative attributions or stereotypes*, meaning the characteristic in question must be perceived as different and bad. Third, the characteristic must be associated with a distinction between "us" (those without the characteristic) and "them" (those with the characteristic), which creates in-group and out-group dynamics. Lastly, those who carry the characteristic must experience *status loss and discrimination* because of their stigmatized characteristic.

How do these criteria relate to the treatment of adolescent parents in the United States? Do the treatment and perceptions of adolescent parenthood in the United States meet the criteria outlined by Pescosolido and Martin (2015) for being stigmatizing? First, given that the term "adolescent parent," which is used to describe those who have given birth or fathered a child at age 19 or younger, exists, adolescent parenthood meets the first criterion of being given a label by society. Second, is being an adolescent parent considered negative? Considering that adolescent parenthood is described as an epidemic and many people (including researchers) highlight the detrimental outcomes associated with adolescent pregnancy, yes, being an adolescent parent is obviously considered negative at the societal level in the United States. Third, is there a distinction between adolescent parents and those who are not adolescent parents, or those that gave birth at an older age? Kelly's (1996) identification of adolescent parents described in the media as the "wrong family" and concerns over adolescent parenthood leading to the destruction of the "traditional family structure" suggest adolescent parenthood meets the third criterion as well. Lastly, do adolescent parents report experiencing status loss and discrimination? Brand, Morrison, and Down's (2014) research highlighting adolescent parents' poor treatment by healthcare workers and their subsequent decision to avoid care suggests that adolescent parents experience discrimination and therefore meet the fourth criterion as well. Therefore, by these criteria, being an adolescent parent is a stigmatizing characteristic in American society.

So how does a socially stigmatized characteristic relate to experiencing stigma on an interpersonal level? The *stigmatization process* helps explain how having a stigmatized characteristic influences individuals such as adolescent parents. According to Goffman (1963), the stigmatization process occurs in three phases. First, an individual meets someone and makes assumptions about their social identity. Generally, these assumptions are unconscious, so that the person is not aware of this process. Second, the individual realizes the person has a characteristic they associated with being "bad" or "wrong." Third, because of this "bad" characteristic, the individual starts to view the other person themselves as being bad. When people equate a "bad" characteristic and a "bad" person, they seek to justify to themselves why this person is inferior. Making this justification involves viewing the person as "other" and less than oneself. Oftentimes, this thought process also leads to feelings of animosity based on those differences, or the belief that the person has a variety of other negative attributes simply because of the category in which they have been placed. Stigmatization occurs when people are made aware they are a member of a stigmatized group because others treat them differently, such as teachers or strangers suggesting those born to adolescent parents will inevitably fail.

Essentially, societal ideals influence how someone communicates with other people, and the way that person communicates their perceptions to others then influences the other person's identity (Mead 1934). For example, if society suggests adolescent pregnancy is immoral and wrong, and someone meets an adolescent parent and communicates to them in a way that suggests they are immoral and wrong due to their status as an adolescent parent, this stigmatization process could influence the identity of the adolescent parent in a negative manner. Therefore, society influences what characteristics are stigmatized, communication is the vehicle through which stigmatization is given life or is communicated to members of the stigmatized group, and over time the communicative interactions that one experiences influence identity development.

Importantly, stigmatization can affect more than just the person with a stigmatized characteristic. Goffman (1963) coined the term *courtesy stigma* to describe what occurs when individuals either related to or sympathetic to a stigmatized individual experience some of the same outcomes as stigmatized individuals, although to a lesser degree. Courtesy stigma is particularly important to consider when examining the role of stigmatization on one's identity because previous research suggests courtesy stigma leads to feelings of blame and guilt. For example, Corrigan and Miller (2004) examined stigma related to mental illness and found some people experienced courtesy stigma because they blamed themselves for their family member's experiences, and others felt like their ill family member's status as stigmatized contaminated them.

The idea of contamination associated with courtesy stigma relates to the epidemic and disease metaphor discussed earlier, in that contamination suggests someone's "disease" has spread to others in the family. Additionally, in Corrigan and Miller's study, those who believed that they personally were to blame for their family members' stigmatization (e.g., a parent might feel at fault that a child is stigmatized for a mental illness believed to be genetic) were worried about being perceived as incompetent, while those who feared contamination from the stigmatized person worried about being perceived as worth less than the average person. Green (2003) found that witnessing a family member being stigmatized can lead to feelings of blame. Their research found that mothers of children with disabilities who felt like their children were being stigmatized felt guilty and ashamed about their children's experience, as if they personally were responsible for the stigmatization.

There are reasons to believe that children of adolescent parents might fear this kind of contamination and/or blame themselves as well. For example, children of adolescent parents may worry others will perceive them as "bad" because their parents were "bad." Additionally, they may believe that their existence in this world has brought shame upon their family and blame themselves for their family's "otherness" status, particularly if the child was born at the height of the adolescent pregnancy "epidemic." The reason why those born during this time period might be particularly at risk for blaming themselves is because their birth during the height of negative societal messaging may result in their being even more likely to hear negative messages about their families or witness their parents being stigmatized during childhood, compared to those born when this negative messaging was not quite as pervasive. The experiences of research participants support the idea that courtesy stigma does take place in families of adolescent parents. For example, when discussing how her own family members communicated the negative societal belief that those born to adolescent parents are destined for failure, interviewee Ashley (37-year-old Caucasian woman whose mother was 16 and father was 20 when she was born) said, "I had to prove to my paternal grandparents that I wasn't going to make the same mistake as my parents because my parents were good parents that raised me right." Importantly, Ashley described the effects of her paternal grandparents' disapproval as particularly influential to how she viewed herself and how she lived her life.

The Influence of Stigmatization of Adolescent Parenthood on Identity

As Ashley's experience shows, the negativity and "otherness" associated with stigmatization can take a toll on individuals who are stigmatized, even for those who experience courtesy stigma. In fact, research has linked stigmatization to lower self-esteem and a higher likelihood of experiencing symptoms of depression (Woodgate et al. 2020). In terms of adolescent pregnancy and parenting specifically, Whitehead (2001) found stigmatization of adolescent parents was associated with feelings of fear, anger, worthlessness, depression, and shame.

The experiences of research participants support the idea that courtesy stigma can be harmful to one's identity. For example, the survey data showed a significant relationship between parental stigmatization and the self-esteem of someone born to adolescent parents, such that those whose parents were stigmatized reported lower self-esteem. Perhaps the most interesting takeaway from the survey data related to stigmatization and identity was that when the authors examined the comparative influence of (1) participants remembering that their parents were stigmatized or (2) participants remembering themselves being stigmatized, only *parental stigmatization* significantly predicted self-esteem. This highlights how influential witnessing one's family member being stigmatized can be to other family members, particularly in the context of adolescent parenthood. The reasoning for why parental stigmatization influenced participant self-esteem while their own experience with stigmatization did not is discussed in-depth in later chapters.

It is important to note that there were circumstances where research participants were not negatively influenced by their parents' stigmatization. This is perfectly encapsulated by an experience that Rebecca, a 47-year-old Caucasian woman whose parents were both 19 when she was born, had with her school principal. During a school conference she attended with her parents, her principal questioned how Rebecca was so intelligent, even asking whether she was raised by her grandparents, trying to come up with an acceptable explanation. Rebecca described this as one of the most stigmatizing experiences she had growing up and was appalled that her intelligence needed an explanation; could she not just *be* smart? While this could have easily had detrimental effects on how she viewed herself and her family, Rebecca said it never caused her to question her abilities.

What determines whether someone adopts their stigma or challenges it? There are a variety of factors that play a role. Whitley and Kermayer's (2008) research found race/culture is influential, with English-speaking European-Canadian adolescent parents being more likely to report being stigmatized, particularly by those they are close to, than those from other ethnic/racial groups. In fact, European-Canadian adolescent parents reported their own parents contributing to the adolescent parent's stigmatization, whereas Afro-Caribbean participants reported never dealing with negative messages about their adolescent parenthood from their own parents.

Research by Edin and Kefalas (2005) and Kiselica (2008) found that those from a low socioeconomic status household tended to describe their adolescent pregnancy as a blessing, or something that has given their life more purpose than it had previously. Importantly, these individuals may still believe the societal stigma against adolescent parenthood exists (and therefore are aware that they are potentially treated differently by those within society), but they do not ascribe to these negative beliefs themselves. Their largely positive views of their pregnancy and the ways it has influenced their life could cause individuals from these low socioeconomic status households to be more likely to reject the social stigma instead of adopting it as part of their identity.

Results from the survey data suggest support of one's family plays a role in whether a person adopts their stigma as part of their identity. For example, prior to adding in demographic information, there was a significant relationship between personal stigmatization and self-esteem, such that when those born to adolescent parents were personally stigmatized because of their parents' age, they had lower self-esteem. However, once demographic and family details were taken into account, the relationship between personal stigmatization and self-esteem decreased significantly. For example, the relationship between personal stigmatization and self-esteem was no longer significant once family cohesion, defined as the emotional bond between family members, was taken into account. Perhaps those individuals who came from cohesive and unified family units were able to work together to overcome the stigma those born to adolescent parents experienced. Rebecca's family environment could help explain why she was not negatively influenced by the interaction with her school principal. She described her family as a three-person unit, and she said she always felt supported by her family. Right after her school principal made the comments, Rebecca's father responded quickly and definitively to defend his daughter's and his own capabilities. Perhaps watching her father defend himself to a critic (the principal) helped Rebecca overcome her stigmatizing experience.

Lastly, family conversations surrounding adolescent parenthood influence whether people personally adopt their stigma as well (Green 2003). For example, if the child's family rejects the stigma of adolescent pregnancy, and the family also describes the birth of the child as a positive experience, the child may be less likely to experience courtesy stigma. Sarah (a 57-year-old Caucasian woman whose mother was 15 and father was 17 when she was born) provides an example of how family conversations can help mitigate negative outcomes associated with family stigmatization. Sarah said she was able to read at an early age, and when she was young she was reading the newspaper and came across an article suggesting those born to adolescent parents who did not finish high school would also not graduate from high school and were destined to be unsuccessful. Her conclusion based on the article was, "No education, no income, your whole life is decided already."

When asked how she was influenced by this experience, Sarah said she was taken aback by the article, but that once her mother and grandmother realized she read the piece, they purposely told her that she was smart and capable of achieving great things. Sarah believed her family members provided her with this positive reinforcement so that she would not accept negative societal messaging about what happens to children of adolescent parents as part of her own self-concept.

Sarah's conversation with her mother and grandmother highlights the ways family conversations can mitigate the damage that stigmatizing experiences can have on one's identity. In Sarah's own words, the main reason why this newspaper article did not make her feel bad about herself and her abilities is because her family stepped in to let her know the article was wrong, or at least that it did not apply to her. The importance of her family's messages to Sarah is not entirely surprising given Mead's assertion that one's identity is influenced by both societal messages and interpersonal messages (like family conversations). Next, the second chapter further discusses the important influence of a specific type of family conversation, family storytelling, in relation to stigma, and unpacks how different types of stories influence people's identity.

NOTE

1. All interviewee names mentioned throughout this manuscript are pseudonyms.

Chapter 2

Family Conversations Surrounding Adolescent Parenthood

How Stigma and Storytelling Relate to Children's Identity

STIGMA AND FAMILY CONVERSATIONS

Interpersonal messages are not only central to forming one's identity, they can also be utilized to either enforce or mitigate experiences of stigmatization. In fact, Goffman (1963) suggests people can avoid the negative outcomes associated with stigma by engaging in communication that reinforces a positive identity. These positive messages could come from anyone, but support from one's family members in the form of positive messages is particularly important. In fact, in their research focused on understanding the stigmatization of alcoholism in families with multiple generations of alcoholics, Haverfield and Theiss (2016) found supportive communication leads to resilience and protection from negative experiences related to stigmatization, such as lower self-esteem and depressive symptoms.

Afifi, Davis, and Merril (2014) found that those from stigmatized family forms are more resilient if they can reframe their stigma as a source of pride or focus on overcoming obstacles. Therefore, it is important to explore the ways families communicate about their stigmatized status, and how this communication relates to the identity of family members. Although the research, discussed previously, highlights the ways communication can be used to mitigate harmful outcomes associated with stigmatization, messages communicated by family members could also end up perpetuating the stigma and therefore ultimately harm family members. For example, it is entirely possible that some families talk about their status as a family with adolescent parents in a negative way and end up stigmatizing themselves and other family members in the process.

This reinforcement of stigmatization via family talk was identified by the research participants in both the survey and interviews. When asked to describe a time they experienced stigmatization, one survey participant said her own aunts would say, "you better watch that girl she gonna [*sic*] get pregnant," reflecting the societal belief that girls born to adolescent parents are more likely to become adolescent parents themselves. Her grandmother also warned her she would become just like her mom, and as a result restricted her ability to play with her friends outside, thinking this restricted play time would lower the likelihood that her granddaughter would get pregnant. Importantly, this particular participant rated the impact of this stigmatizing family messaging on her as 100 on a 0–100 scale.

Ultimately, many types of family messages have the potential to help reduce the harm of stigmatization or reinforce that harm, but the most influential family messages are likely those that people remember in great detail over time. Two types of influential messages that researchers have previously connected to identity formation in families are memorable messages and family narratives. *Memorable messages* are verbal messages people remember, that are heard relatively early in life, and that individuals consider influential in some way (Knapp, Stohl, and Reardon 1981). The messages from the previously discussed participant's aunts and grandmother are perfect examples of memorable messages, as they are messages that have remained influential to this individual over time, even into adulthood.

The second type of message, *family narratives*, are stories told within and/or about the family that reflect what family members find significant in their lives and/or the life of the family as a whole (Stone 1988). According to Fiese and Winter (2009), "Family stories are verbal accounts of personal experiences that are important to the family, [which] depict rules of interaction, reflect beliefs about the trustworthiness of relationships, and impact values connected to larger social institutions" (p. 626). Researchers believe family stories communicate the world of family members, including the culture each family has created, the family's values, and the identity of either the family as a whole or as individual family members (Langellier and Peterson 2006).

Even though both *memorable messages* and *family stories* can play a role in how people manage experiences with stigmatization and how they think about themselves, this book focuses specifically on family stories. This choice was made for two main reasons. First, Galvin (2006) identified family stories as a central way for members of discourse-dependent families to manage their "otherness" status and legitimize their family as real. Second, multiple areas of research (on stigma, on family forms that are considered different than the norm, and on interpersonal messages that influence identity) focus on family storytelling, suggesting storytelling is central to all the processes examined here.

Importantly, there are many different types of stories families tell and while many stories could influence the identity of those born to adolescent parents, certain stories are more likely to be directly related to identity formation of others, particularly because of their stigmatized status. For example, because the stigmatization of adolescent parenthood is related to the birth and/or existence of the child, stories surrounding the child's conception, birth, or overall existence are most relevant. Stories about conception are related to what researchers call *reproductive stories*, or those stories focused on how a child came to be (Nordqvist 2021). *Birth stories* or *entrance stories* are those focused on a child's entrance into the family (Kranstuber and Koenig Kellas 2011). Previous research has supported the idea that reproductive and birth/entrance stories are significantly related to the identity of children (Kranstuber and Koenig Kellas 2011; Nordqvist 2021). The authors termed those stories focused on one's existence *origin stories*, and they tend to focus on what happened after a parent found out they were pregnant. For example, origin stories might reflect how a family member reacted to news of the pregnancy or how parents themselves dealt with the news. These stories are therefore particularly relevant to processes of stigmatization, as they may reflect the first time the adolescent parents are stigmatized and/or how the parents reacted to that potential stigmatization.

Because *reproductive*, *birth/entrance*, and *origin* stories are most likely to be tied to identity formation, they are the stories the authors focused on during data collection. In survey responses and interviews, research participants were asked to reflect on the most influential stories they were told surrounding their conception, birth, or existence and discuss how those stories influenced how they viewed themselves. Therefore, any story-related survey and interview data discussed throughout the remainder of this book reflects reproductive, birth/entrance, and/or origin stories participants identified as being particularly influential to them throughout their lives.

Discourse-Dependent Families, Stigma, and Family Stories

As previously mentioned, the concept of discourse-dependent families refers to an approach to understanding families that focuses on how family members use communication to develop close bonds and manage group identity. Families that scholars refer to as *discourse-dependent* are those that must engage in more communication both within and outside the family more frequently than others. Importantly, families could be considered discourse-dependent for numerous reasons, including but not limited to having family ties to one another that are not visibly obvious (e.g., adopted children of a different race than the adoptive parents or stepfamilies) or having a family form that is less accepted socially (e.g., same-sex families) (Galvin 2006). Galvin identified eight different communication strategies discourse-dependent families use to manage their "otherness": four external, for communicating with outsiders, and four internal, for communication within the family.

The first external management strategy is *labeling*, which refers to identifying family relationships when referring family members to those outside the family. For example, when introducing one's parents to outsiders, someone might say, "This is Jim, my father and Meredyth, my mother." The second tactic is *explaining*, which refers to making family relationships understandable to outsiders by either giving reasons for the relationship or clarifying how the family relationship works. For example, the individual from the previous example might say, "I know it's hard to believe they are my parents; they were teenagers when I was born, so we're not that far apart in age." The third tactic, *legitimizing*, refers to positioning one's familial relationships as real and genuine. For example, if the family members encounter someone who says, "There's no way she's your daughter . . . you look more like siblings!" the daughter might respond with, "Yeah, I know, but they actually are my parents. I promise, my mother gave birth to me!" The last external boundary management tactic is *defending*, or shielding oneself from an attack on one's family form, and it tends to reflect strong feelings such as frustration or annoyance. For example, if a family member hears someone criticize their family form, they might respond by saying, "It is none of your business" (Galvin 2006).

Galvin (2006) also describes four internal boundary management tactics, which refer to processes family members engage in with each other to maintain a sense of "family-ness" within the family. Although all four (naming, discussing, ritualizing, and narrating) internal boundary management tactics[1] are important to discourse-dependent families, one stands out as being particularly relevant to families of adolescent parents: *narrating*, or telling stories that help the family and family members develop their identity (Galvin 2006). For example, adolescent parents might tell their child a story explaining that they were conceived on purpose to show that their family, and the child themselves, is not a mistake. Importantly, Galvin suggests the particular language utilized in narratives helps to determine the type of influence a story will have on individuals within the family.

Stigma tends to be naturally associated with discourse-dependent families because the definition of a discourse-dependent family specifically relates to families that do not fit the "norm." In fact, according to Galvin (2006), the more different the family is from whatever society considers "normal" and the more ambiguous family members' ties to one another, the more discourse-dependent the family is considered. For example, a stepfamily with members of the same race and with a typical age gap between parental figures and children would be less discourse-dependent than a stepfamily with members of various races and perhaps one parental figure that is close in age to one or more children.

This increased level of discourse-dependence also leads to a higher likelihood of having to engage in the boundary management tactics Galvin identified. For instance, because the second stepfamily described earlier does not look like a "normal" family, members of this family would be more likely to need to explain their family to outsiders and to themselves. This also means members of discourse-dependent families might be more likely to engage in narrating than members of other families, particularly narrating as a tactic to manage or mitigate their "otherness," that is, their stigma. In fact, Huisman (2014) found stories focused on identity management, which are defined as stories that reflect the culture of the family itself (i.e., providing information about what it means to be a member of the family) or illustrate the identity of one family member, can sometimes be used to try to ascertain that families with a stigmatizing characteristic are perceived as acceptable to others.

Before moving on, it is important to consider whether families of adolescent parents should be identified as high in discourse-dependence. There are a variety of reasons to think they are, suggesting storytelling could be an important process in these families. For example, because there is a smaller than "normal" age difference between parents and their children, it is possible that family members would need to explain their parent-child relationship to outsiders who may assume they are siblings or romantic partners rather than parents and children. Furthermore, Afifi, Davis, and Merril (2014) suggest the stigmatization adolescent parents and their families experience, particularly unwed adolescent parents, means that family members must legitimize their family form to outsiders, another common experience for members of discourse-dependent families.

An analysis of survey data gives more evidence considering whether those born to adolescent parents themselves have engaged in the boundary management tactics outlined by Galvin (2006), and if so, how frequently they engaged in each.[2] Not only did participants report engaging in all five boundary management tactics measured in the survey, but they were most likely to report engaging in explaining (average of 3.01 on a 1–5 scale) and narrating (average of 2.97 on a 1–5 scale), compared to legitimizing (average of 2.56 on a 1–5 scale), labeling (average of 2.36 on a 1–5 scale), and defending (average of 2.35 on a 1–5 scale).[3] These findings highlight the frequent use of explaining and narrating boundary management tactics in families of adolescent parents and provide evidence that narrating is common in these families.

Furthermore, data from both the survey and interviews from the study utilized for this book support the idea that storytelling was used by children of adolescent parents to mitigate stigma and help members understand their family form. For example, using survey methodology, the authors examined whether people who reported their parents were stigmatized due to their status as an adolescent parent were more likely to report having family members who engaged in storytelling. Even after controlling for a variety of other factors including participant ethnicity, the relationship between one's parents (at birth, while growing up, and currently), participant education, education of one's parents (at birth, while growing up, and currently), the number of people in one's household growing up, family closeness levels, family cohesion levels, whether the survey participant themselves felt personally stigmatized due to their parents' status as an adolescent parent, and *whether one's parent was stigmatized significantly predicted the use of storytelling in one's family*. In other words, if someone reported that their parent was stigmatized because they had a child as an adolescent, they were also more likely to report that their family engaged in storytelling frequently.

Findings from the interview data highlight how storytelling was specifically utilized as a way family members responded to stigmatizing experiences. Many of the interviewees described their parents talking to them about their *ability* and the importance of their *presence on this earth* in response to either real or imagined stigmatization. Sarah's (a 57-year-old Caucasian woman whose mother was 15 and father was 17 when she was born) experience provides a good example of this. Her mother constantly told her stories reflecting the idea that she was smart and capable of achieving great things after Sarah read a newspaper article suggesting those born to adolescent parents were doomed to a life of failure. Additionally, one participant, Kiana (a 19-year-old African American woman whose mother was 18 and father was 19 when she was born) said her mother always told her a story reflecting that she was on this earth because God had a purpose for her and she was not a mistake. She said this message was important to her identity because her existence and purpose were something that she grappled with as a child.

Together, the results from both the survey and the interviews highlighted previously support the idea that storytelling and narration is indeed an important communication tool for families of adolescent parents and suggest these stories have lasting effects on how those born to adolescent parents see themselves. The next step is understanding *why and how* these stories influence the identity of those born to adolescent parents.

Family Storytelling and Identity in Discourse-Dependent Families

According to Becker (1997), people have the tendency to compare themselves to what is normal, and when they believe some aspect of their lives is not normal, they internalize their differentness and do everything they can to correct it. The tendency to focus on one's differentness can have a variety of negative implications for the individual's well-being, including negatively affecting their self-esteem and, consequently, their identity. Therefore, those from discourse-dependent families may use positive stories to decrease the likelihood that their family members develop a negative identity.

For example, one of the commonly held beliefs about adolescent pregnancy is that getting pregnant is a "mistake." If children internalize the belief that their birth was a mistake, they might start to believe *they themselves* are mistakes. Such beliefs can have detrimental effects on their self-worth and identity. However, family stories centered on the children being wanted can aid in avoiding internalizing these negative self-thoughts. To illustrate, as mentioned earlier, in her survey and interview responses Kiana noted that the most influential story her mother told her while growing up focused on the idea that she had a purpose and that she was on this earth for a reason. When discussing this story and its implications for her identity, she said, "Sometimes I feel like maybe I was a mistake, but then my mom [made] sure to reinforce that if God wanted me to be here that's why [I'm here]." She said she has carried this message with her throughout her life and continues to remember that "mistakes" are part of God's plan. Kiana's story served as a way that family members helped to negate harmful thoughts that Kiana may have had about herself and her place in the world. Kiana's example shows how family stories regarding one's birth have the *potential* to influence people's identity.

Stories are so influential to people's identity that, according to Koenig Kellas and Kranstuber Horstman's (2015) Communicated Narrative Sensemaking theory (CNSM), the stories people hear about themselves become adopted as *part* of their identity. Furthermore, McAdams (1993) suggests individuals use these stories to help them develop their own personal myth, which reflects one's personal truth, identity, and values, and is often influenced by the information children learn about themselves from family members. In fact, Stone (1988) claims that people's deepest sense of who they are comes from the stories families tell them about themselves. So, stories influence people's identity, but exactly how does this process occur?

Two important characteristics of stories that help explain the influence stories have on people's identity are the tone of the story and the ways in which story listeners perceive and interpret the story. In terms of *tone*, Hayden, Singer, and Chrisler (2006) suggest stories can be used to paint a certain type of picture for families and individual family members. For example, stories can have a *positive tone* by being told in a way that downplays potential negatives of being different and highlights the positive aspects of one's life events, such as overcoming difficulty. Stories used in this manner have been shown to provide positive reinforcement and positively affect one's self-esteem (Hayden, Singer, and Chrisler 2006). This is what happened to Kiana when the story told by her mother emphasized that she was not a mistake.

An example of the negative influence of tone comes from survey responses. For example, consider the tone of this story reported by one survey participant,

> I was told that my mom had many plans to work in the medical field, but because of her "mistake" she had to ignore her acceptance to schools and get a full-time job to support raising me. After a while she started taking night classes, but along with this started using speed, and in no time she was again unable to attend school and apparently this largely lands on my shoulders. (31-year-old male whose mother was 19 and father was 18 when he was born).

Not only is this story clearly negative in tone, but it also suggests hearing this story influenced him to feel like he was to blame for his mother's choices. This person's story is drastically different from Kiana's story and highlights the various experiences those born to adolescent parents have when it comes to storytelling.

Although tone is important, so too is the way in which story listeners *perceive the valence* of the stories they are told. In some instances, while the storyteller may intend to tell a positive and helpful story, the listener may interpret the story differently and ultimately walk away with a negative message. For example, one interviewee, Emerson (a 23-year-old Caucasian woman whose mother was 17 and father was 19 when she was born), talked about a story her mother told her focusing on how her birth and entrance into the world saved her mother. While this story might sound positive from the outside, Emerson described this story as extremely detrimental to her. She said it put too much pressure on her and ultimately was one reason she became estranged from her mother over time. Unfortunately, Emerson's mother's attempt to provide a positive story to her daughter to counter negative perceptions of adolescent parenthood was not effective. Although Emerson's mother had good intentions, Emerson interpreted the story differently than her mother, and the story became toxic for her.

IN THEIR OWN WORDS: THE INFLUENCE OF STORIES ON THE IDENTITY OF THOSE BORN TO ADOLESCENT PARENTS

To further understand why and how various stories influence those born to adolescent parents, it is necessary to hear from the children of adolescent parents themselves and explore any potential patterns concerning how they describe the influence of storytelling on their identity. A thematic analysis of conversations with interview participants revealed two major themes related to the various ways stories influenced the identity of those born to adolescent parents: *identity support* and *identity struggle*. The theme of *identity support* is associated with stories that helped interviewees to know that they were chosen, wanted, planned, and/or desired, and these stories had positive influences on their identity. Based on the interviewee's descriptions, family members purposely told these stories to participants to ensure they did not think of themselves as a mistake. Kiana's (a 19-year-old African American woman whose mother was 18 and father was 19 when she was born) story about being on this earth because God had a purpose for her is a perfect example of this. Most of the time, these stories succeeded in providing positive reinforcement to the child's identity.

A perfect example that highlights why positive stories were so influential comes from Rebecca (a 47-year-old Caucasian woman whose parents were both 19 when she was born). She said her reproductive story focused on how her birth was planned and desired, and she even referred to her story as the "spite baby story." According to her story, her parents got pregnant on purpose so that they could get married at a young age, despite the reservations of her paternal grandmother. When describing her story, she said,

> When they were dating my father said, "I'm going to marry this girl." My grandmother said, "No, you can't. . . . I'm not going to allow that to happen." Whether or not they got pregnant on purpose I don't know if that part is true, but it certainly enabled them to get married without her raising a fuss.

Rebecca's "spite baby story" illustrated to her that she never has to question whether she was wanted because her existence gave her parents exactly what they wanted, to be together. Rebecca was one interviewee who really did not talk about struggling with low self-worth or identity-related issues despite her parents experiencing stigmatization from both outsiders and her own extended family. In Rebecca's interview she said her grandmother never wanted her parents to get married and told her father that if they got married and had children too early, he would not get a good education. This story highlights Rebecca's grandmother's belief that having children early would ruin her dad's life, aligning with the negative societal narrative about adolescent parenthood. Although these stigmatizing messages about her family life could have harmed Rebecca, the story that she was told about being chosen and wanted superseded the negative messaging from her grandmother and helped her maintain a positive outlook on her family and her identity.

The second theme, *identity struggle*, related to negative implications for identity caused by the stories interviewees heard. For example, Erin (a 22-year-old Caucasian woman whose mother was 18 and father was 19 when she was born) heard contradicting stories from her family members. Some family members told her that she was unplanned and an accident, but her mother's story was different. Erin said her mother had conceived before becoming pregnant with Erin, but her mother chose to terminate her previous pregnancies. Erin was the first baby her mother carried to term, and her mother always made sure to tell Erin that she was wanted, that she chose to carry her to term, and that she chose to keep her. Although a story with this focus may seem as if it would be positive, for Erin it led to a lot of frustration and mixed emotions. She said the contradicting stories from family members led her to conclude that her mother was lying and telling her what she thought would be helpful instead of the truth. She said, "She had good intentions . . . she told me these stories and they just made the bad ones truer. . . . I would have preferred the truth." Importantly, and most directly related to the placement of this story in the *identity struggle* theme, she also said that the stories she heard growing up negatively influenced her self-esteem and that she ended up having to go to therapy to work through the issues they caused.

Examples like Erin's are important to highlight because they show how nuanced the connection between stigmatizing experiences, storytelling, and one's identity can be. In fact, support for the idea that stories others tell with the intent to have a positive tone (like Erin's mother) do not always have the intended positive effect on one's identity was also found in the survey data. When analyzing these data, the authors found that, although parental experiences with stigmatization predicted a higher frequency of storytelling in one's family, contrary to predictions, hearing a positive story from one's family members did not lead to higher self-esteem. At first, this finding might be counterintuitive, but when it is considered within the context of experiences like Erin's, it highlights how families may engage in storytelling with the intent to mitigate stigma, but this intent does not always align with the valence of the impact their stories have on their children.

Almost every interviewee whose story exhibited the *identity struggle* theme talked about the stories they heard growing up leading to a sense of guilt and burden, which ultimately made them believe they had to prove their worth to others to alleviate their guilt and ease the burden they caused. For example, as mentioned in chapter 1, Ashley (a 37-year-old Caucasian woman whose mother was 16 and father was 20 when she was born) discussed a story from her father's side of the family that focused on the idea that her mother got pregnant young and out of wedlock and concluded Ashley was destined for a life of failure. When discussing her desire to always be her best, Ashley said,

> I do believe my parents' approval has been a driving force for me. . . . I had to prove to my paternal grandparents that I wasn't going to make the same mistake as my parents because my parents were good parents that raised me right.

It was clear that the story Ashley heard from the paternal side of her family made her feel as if she had something to prove.

Importantly, everyone who mentioned experiencing feelings of guilt and burden related to their identity as a child of adolescent parents also clarified that their parents never explicitly told them that they were a burden, or that they needed to prove their worth. Instead, as they reflected on their experiences, they heard certain stories as children and then surmised that, based on what they were told, they were a burden to their family. Many spoke of participating in therapy, engaging in extensive self-reflection, and/or using religion to cope with and work through the self-blame they placed on themselves as children.

The experiences related to stigmatization and storytelling and their relationship with identity, particularly as they relate to guilt and burden, are complicated and must always be understood in consideration of both their family environment and societal expectations/messages (i.e., stigmatization) surrounding adolescent pregnancy. Therefore, chapter 3 explores experiences of guilt and burden further by examining interview responses in more depth to help explain *why* and *how* stigmatization and storytelling may lead to feeling guilty in the first place. Following that discussion, an explanation of the coping mechanisms those born to adolescent parents reported using to help them manage their feelings of guilt and burden is discussed in chapter 4.

NOTES

1. The internal three tactics not focused on in this study are defined here: *Naming* refers to what family members call each other. This process refers to both legal names and how family members refer to one another more generally. *Discussing* refers to identifying issues the family could experience and attempting to resolve them together (Galvin, 2006). Lastly, *ritualizing* refers to deciding what family rituals to engage in and which to end (Galvin, 2006).

2. Because the study was focused on storytelling specifically, the authors asked about all four external boundary management tactics defined by Galvin, but the only internal boundary management tactic they asked about was storytelling.

3. To determine whether frequency of engagement in each boundary management tactic was significantly different from the other tactics, the authors calculated 95% confidence intervals around the mean score for each boundary management tactic measured (labeling, explaining, legitimizing, defending, and narrating). Each confidence interval was then compared to the others to see whether the confidence interval of one tactic overlapped with the others. If an overlap occurred, that meant there was no significant difference in how frequently participants reported engaging in those two tactics. This is how the authors determined people were more likely to engage in explaining and narrating compared to the other tactics.

Chapter 3

The Burden Experienced by Those Born to Adolescent Parents

As chapter 2 pointed out, a variety of research has linked storytelling to identity development (Kranstuber and Koenig Kellas 2011; McAdams 1993), and the data from the study utilized for this book verifies that storytelling is a common communication activity in families of adolescent parents, as well as influential to the identity development of those born to adolescent parents. The next important step in understanding the influence of storytelling on identity development is to explore the specific ways stigmatization of adolescent parenthood and family storytelling combine to influence the identity of those born to adolescent parents. Because the conversations with interviewees provided the richest description of this somewhat complex connection, this chapter focuses on interview responses participants provided that elaborated on their experiences as the child of an adolescent parent and on how the stories they were told affected them throughout their lives. Importantly, interviewees were asked to focus their responses on the *reproductive*, *birth/entrance*, or *origin* story they identified as being most influential to their lives.

This chapter also focuses on unpacking the experiences of those individuals whose stories were associated with the theme of *identity struggle* or stories that had a negative influence on individuals as defined in chapter 2. This is because a common pattern emerged for these individuals in particular, which involved struggles they witnessed as children influencing how they interpreted the stories they were told. For example, all the interviewees talked openly about their parents struggling in some way, but those who heard stories that negatively influenced their identity talked about internalizing their parents' struggles and feeling guilty about their parents' circumstances. Those who felt guilty also described feeling like a burden to their parents and believing that their birth, and really their overall existence, was what caused their parents' struggles. As a result of this guilt and burden, it was common for people to talk about believing they had to prove their worth. Importantly, many of the struggles people referenced are related to common negative social beliefs about adolescent pregnancy/parenthood, ultimately relating to the stigmatization of adolescent pregnancy. This chapter therefore seeks to explain how and why experiencing stigmatization and hearing stories specifically associated with *identity struggle* led to feelings of guilt and burden and the belief that one must prove their worth for interviewees.

Given the harmful effects of drawing conclusions from research that focuses solely on the negative outcomes associated with being born to adolescent parents described in chapter 1, it is important to clarify that those born to adolescent parents are not a monolith, and their experiences are not all the same. Not every person interviewed described experiencing feelings of guilt and a resulting burden (e.g., those who heard stories of *identity support*), but the experience of guilt was common enough that this connection was an important part of the story the data were telling. Therefore, what follows exhibits the open and honest reflections of interviewees but is not meant to suggest the lives of those born to adolescent parents are filled with harm and negativity. In fact, many (but not all) of those who discussed feeling guilty and being a burden also talked about positive aspects of their childhood and their relationship with their parents.

THE IMPORTANCE OF PARENTAL STRUGGLE

All interviewees (regardless of whether the family stories they identified positively or negatively influenced them) described witnessing their parents go through some sort of struggle. These difficulties included (1) feeling as if their parents were unable to reach or had a difficult time reaching their potential, (2) witnessing relationship issues between their parents, and (3) experiencing familial economic instability.

As interviewees described these situations, it became clear that the experience of witnessing their parents struggle clearly had an important influence on them, even into adulthood. For example, Ashley (a 37-year-old Caucasian woman whose mother was 16 and father was 20 when she was born) was a perfect example of someone who felt as if her parent was unable to reach their potential. When describing her childhood, Ashley consistently referred to the opportunities her mother had to give up. Ashley commented,

> My mom didn't finish high school because of my birth, and it held her back for years until she decided to get her diploma through an at-home school through the mail. My mom is an amazing woman and I think she has tremendous potential that she never got to see fully blossom.

This is a theme Ashley continued to talk about in the interview, and it became clear she believed her birth held her mother back.

There were a few interviewees who talked about the hardships that resulted from watching their parents go through relationship struggles. Naomi (a 24-year-old African American woman whose mother was 18 and father was 19 when she was born) explained, "[G]rowing up I was the person who kind of saw the issues [my parents] had . . . trying to make it work for the kids." Naomi also said that witnessing her parents' relationship issues encouraged her to step in and help her mother. She said, "I didn't always try to fix it necessarily, I guess I just didn't know how to do anything like that, but I definitely tried to be helpful." Her description of these events suggests watching her parents struggle in their relationship led her to believe that she had to step in at a young age and try to help in some way. Naomi's feelings reflect quite a hefty responsibility for a young child and could have had detrimental effects on her relationship with her parents later. In fact, she said witnessing these struggles and seeing everything her mother did to support her and her siblings were major reasons why she did not really have a relationship with her father while she was growing up. Although she has tried to repair the relationship with her father as an adult, they are still not as close as she and her mother are.

Lastly, economic struggles were a particular type of struggle commonly reported by interviewees. For example, when reflecting on the shame that his father experienced because he was not able to afford Christmas presents for his kids, Manuel (a 35-year-old Hispanic male whose parents were both 17 when he was born) said,

> My father is a construction worker, so two things would typically happen; summers would be fine, busy, he's working, money's good. But then come winter, work gets slow . . . my family was on welfare . . . [they] definitely felt shame about it.

The influence of the economic struggles Manuel's family experienced surfaced throughout his interview, with Manuel explaining that his father always told him how much easier life would have been if he had waited to have children later in life.

The reason the struggles the interviewees described previously were so important to their identity development was because, for many, they identified themselves as the cause of the struggles they witnessed. Once they saw their parents struggle, they equated the struggle to the fact that their parents were so young when they were born and then surmised that if it were not for their birth, their parents' lives would not be so difficult. Although they clearly were not responsible for their conception and the resulting pregnancy, they still felt *personally* responsible for ways in which their birth made their parents' lives harder. Due to this perceived responsibility, they believed that as children they needed to do something to prove their existence was worth their parents' struggles. For example, as Ashley reflected on her parents' struggles, she said, "there were times I felt like a burden because I felt that I held my parents back from what they could have become."

Unfortunately, this personal sense of responsibility that resulted from witnessing parental struggles also became a filter that influenced how interviewees interpreted the stories they were told as children. Ultimately, stories that interviewees interpreted negatively (i.e., those categorized as *identity struggle*) ended up reinforcing their belief that they were responsible for their parents' hardships, resulting in feelings of guilt. But why did these children of adolescent parents feel guilty for situations they had no control over?

Parental Struggle and Guilt

Guilt is described as a moral emotion that involves negative evaluations of one's behavior. It is commonly conflated with shame, which, although related, is a distinct emotional experience (Tangney 1995). The easiest way to distinguish between guilt and shame is to think of guilt as the belief that someone did a "bad" thing, whereas shame is the belief that one is a "bad" person. Importantly, while both guilt and shame have been linked to outcomes like low self-esteem, guilt is generally associated with more positive outcomes such as self-improvement and self-forgiveness, but shame is consistently linked with more negative outcomes such as criticizing oneself and avoidance of failure (Wayne Leach 2017). Essentially, guilt causes people to think about how they can improve, while shame tends to lead to negative thinking, pessimism, avoidance, and general inaction.

When examining the interviewees' responses, the choice to use the term *guilt* instead of *shame* was made only after comparing the definition of shame and guilt to the interviewees' own words to see which aligned best with their experiences. Guilt seemed more aligned with the experience of interviewees because no one really talked about getting stuck in patterns of negative thinking and inaction. Instead, it was much more common for interviewees to describe their guilt and feelings of burden as motivating them to succeed and achieve in an attempt to prove their parents' struggles were "worth it." Struggling to show that they were "worth it" can be perceived as the behavior they engaged in to assuage their guilt.

So how did guilt function for those born to adolescent parents? In this context, the "bad thing" interviewees "did" was to be born, and it was their existence in this world that made them feel guilty. The belief that the "bad thing" that occurred was one's birth is perfectly encapsulated in Manuel's description of feeling guilty about his parents' relationship struggles because he knew they only married because he was born and Ashley's admission that she took responsibility for her mother's struggles and therefore felt like a burden in her mother's life.

Even though taking responsibility for their parents' circumstances might not seem logical, it is common for children to take on responsibility for events out of their control and therefore feel guilty. For example, Weisz and Stipek (1982) found it is normal for children to overestimate their own responsibility for factors that are not actually in their control, and Shaver (1985) found that when people blame themselves for something out of their control, they are likely to feel guilty.

The ideas outlined in research by Weisz and Stipek and Shaver relate to what is termed *self-blame*. Self-blame refers to believing that internal and permanent characteristics of oneself are to blame for a negative situation (Kouros, Wee, Carson, and Ekas 2020). Remember that guilt refers to the belief that one did a "bad thing." If that "bad thing" caused others harm, then feeling guilty would lead to blaming oneself for that harm. Research by Kornhaber, Childs, and Cleary (2018) supports this idea. They explain that because guilt is associated with one's behavior, guilt can be exacerbated by concerns about how one's behavior has affected other people. Therefore, when one blames themselves for someone else's circumstances, they are more likely to feel personally guilty about that other person's particular circumstances as well. So, for those born to adolescent parents, when they witness their parents struggle, they perceive being born as a negative behavior they engaged in and thus conclude as children that they are to blame for their parents' circumstances.

This tendency for children to take responsibility for situations outside of their control is likely a result of children's proclivity to interpret life events from their own perspective. For example, according to Piaget's theory of cognitive development (Piaget 1970), young children (around 3–7 years old) are naturally egocentric, meaning they see the world through their own eyes and believe everyone else has the same perspective that they do. This phenomenon means that children are unable to think from perspectives other than their own (Kesserling and Müller 2011). Being egocentric influences how people make sense of the world, including how they explain cause-and-effect relationships; therefore, when a child's focus is on themselves, it is common for them to see themselves as the cause of struggles within their family.

The cognitive process can be further explained by attribution theory (Heider 1958). According to this theory, humans act as naïve scientists who seek to make sense of the world around them by explaining why people behave in certain ways and why certain events occur. An important part of the attribution process occurs when people try to determine the locus of causality or the reason for why events occur, particularly for their and others' behavior.

The locus of causality can be internal (within the person) or external (due to outside circumstances) (Heider 1958), and in the case of those born to adolescent parents, interview responses suggest guilt and self-blame occur because they make an internal attribution for the cause of their family's struggles.

Heider (1958) also developed several levels of responsibility that individuals apply to themselves when determining the locus of causality, but only two closely relate to the experiences those born to adolescent parents described in their interviews. The first is termed *association*, which refers to a situation in which a person is considered responsible because he or she was *associated* with a negative outcome although he or she was not the *causal* agent of the event. An example of *association* from the interviews would be Sarah's (a 57-year-old Caucasian woman whose mother was 15 and father was 17 when she was born) realization that she took responsibility for her parents having difficult lives, even admitting that she had to "prove it was okay [she] was alive." Sarah never said that she was the cause of her parent's struggle, but specifically mentioned feeling responsible; she was associated with their negative outcome.

The second level of responsibility relevant to interviewees' experiences is termed *commission*, which occurs when someone is considered responsible because their behavior *caused* a negative outcome for another person, even though he or she did not intend nor foresee the outcome resulting from their behavior (Mongeau, Hale, and Alles 1994). An example of the commission would be Manuel's belief that his birth caused his parents' struggles. In 'this context, the "behavior" Manuel engaged in was being born, and it was his birth (which was perceived as negative) that he believed caused negative outcomes for his parents. Importantly, unlike Sarah, Manuel did talk about himself and his existence as being problematic and the catalyst for his parents' negative experiences. For example, he said, "It would kill him to hear that, but I got the sense that I made things harder." For both Sarah and Manuel, as well as others who described taking responsibility for their parents' struggles, this act of taking personal responsibility then tainted their interpretation of the stories they were told as children, which will be further discussed in the next section.

THE RELATIONSHIP BETWEEN STRUGGLE, GUILT, SELF-BLAME, AND STORY INTERPRETATION

Based on the description of interviewees, as the authors examined their responses to try to understand how the stories they identified as most influential affected them, taking experiences with familial struggle, guilt, and self-blame into account, the authors came to an important conclusion. It was not necessarily the content of the story itself that influenced each person's identity development, instead it was *the story they themselves created* to understand why their parents struggled, with this understanding of familial struggles serving as a filter for how they interpreted the stories they were told as children. Essentially, the self-narrative they create based on the attributions they made about their parents' experiences is really what leads to damaging beliefs about themselves and their worth. Previous research has linked attributions and levels of responsibility to feelings of guilt (McGraw 1987). Overall, then, it is not surprising that the result of the act of taking responsibility for their parents' circumstances is the child feeling guilty.

Information provided by Manuel and Ashley about how their parents' struggles influenced them helps to highlight the ways internalizing one's parents' struggles can serve as a filter for how one interprets the stories they are told by their family members. As previously mentioned, Manuel's family struggled financially. His parents also struggled with their relationship, and these two circumstances influenced how Manuel interpreted stories told by his father about how much harder life was because his parents had children at a young age. When talking about the influence of these stories, he explained that his parents believed they had to marry but really did not want to be together, and he felt responsible for them being "forced" into a marriage. He said, "It would kill [my father] to hear that, but I got the sense that I made things harder. My parents ultimately did get divorced . . . but I know . . . without a doubt that they got married because of me." Unfortunately, Ashley's belief that she was a burden and held her parents back was reinforced by stories from her grandmother concerning how much her mother gave up in order to raise her and jokes her father made about what he could have been doing with his life if it were not for her mother getting pregnant so young. Importantly, Ashley clearly stated her father never said anything was her fault and she knew her father was joking, but with her mother's struggles and her father's jokes as context, she could not help but take personal responsibility for their circumstances when she heard stories from her grandmother.

Story Interpretation and Identity Development

The above-mentioned experiences show that the struggles interviewees witnessed as children commonly influenced the way they interpreted stories they were told, and ultimately the observation of these struggles was connected to feelings of burden and personal responsibility. This sense of burden and personal responsibility then took a toll on the identity of those born to adolescent parents. For example, Manuel (a 35-year-old Hispanic male whose parents were both 17 when he was born) said,

When you're a 10-year-old and you're already getting . . . it seems like an annual thing of getting told like, "Having kids is hard, you should wait," and you're like, "Oh, I'm a kid, and you're saying having kids are hard. I must be hard." And I don't think I really . . . Sadly, I don't think I really got over that until I started my PhD program.

Erin (22-year-old Caucasian woman whose mother was 18 and father was 19 when she was born) also mentioned feeling like the burden of responsibility she carried put too much pressure on her shoulders to be perfect and have an important purpose in life, ultimately contributing to her experience with depression and need to see a therapist.

The stigmatization of adolescent parenthood is key to understanding why the interpretation of the stories one is told influences the identity of those born to adolescent parents. It is common for members of stigmatized families, or those with a family member who is stigmatized, to blame themselves for their family's/family member's hardships. According to Muhlbauer (2002), guilt often occurs when people internalize their stigma or the stigma of their family members. Internalizing stigma occurs when someone accepts the negative messages associated with their stigmatized characteristic, or the stigmatized characteristic of a loved one, and applies it to themselves, and it is often associated with believing one deserves to be treated badly. Muhlbauer examined how guilt and stigmatization work for those related to someone stigmatized because of a mental illness. The results showed that family members who internalized the stigma associated with the mental illness of their family member reported they felt helpless as they watched their family member experience stigmatization, and this inability to help is ultimately what made them feel guilty.

Muhlbauer's research was focused on health-related stigma and not the stigma associated with adolescent pregnancy, but comments made by interviewees suggest that the basic premise of her research still holds in this context. The connection between internalized stigma and guilt was reflected in the experiences of some interviewees. For example, when explaining how the stigmatization of adolescent parenthood influenced him, Manuel said,

But when you do realize that you're born to young parents, there's this sense of, "Oh, my parents did something wrong." And, too, "I'm the reason they did something wrong." It's a weird, for lack of a better word, kind of a shitty experience.

So why does internalized stigma lead to guilt and self-blame for those born to adolescent parents? Because if those born to adolescent parents internalize the stigma associated with adolescent pregnancy, it means they have adopted the belief (to at least some extent) that adolescent parenthood is bad, and that it is their birth that caused their parents' "bad" label. Because being stigmatized involves being treated negatively by others due to one's stigmatized status, those born to adolescent parents then are more likely to see their parents' negative struggles resulting from the fact that they had a child at a young age. As described earlier, when children are faced with these messages and internalize them as children because of the egocentric way they process and make sense of situations, their takeaway from witnessing the stigmatization is that they are the source of their parents' issues. Had they not been born, their parents would not have been given the "bad" label of an adolescent parent and therefore would not have been treated so poorly.

Importantly, Woodgate et al. (2020) examined the stigmatization of anxiety disorders and found that internalizing stigma also leads to a sense of burden and/or worthlessness. For example, one participant from Woodgate's study talked about how they always felt like a burden and felt worthless and deserving of any social rejection they experienced. Woodgate's finding was reflected in the stories of this study's interviewees as well. In interviews, as those born to adolescent parents explained the responsibility and resulting guilt they felt about their parents' struggles, they often reported that their guilt caused them to feel like a burden to their parents. For example, Ashley (a 37-year-old Caucasian woman whose mother was 16 and father was 20 when she was born) mentioned that her grandmother would tell her stories about how hard her mother's life was. As Ashley heard these stories, she internalized the blame for her mother's struggles and believed it was her fault that her mother did not reach her potential. She specifically mentioned feeling like she was a burden to her parents and held them back. Additionally, Erin even felt so guilty about burdening her parents that she admitted to feeling a little relieved when her parents took back an offer to pay for her college. She said, "I felt terrible that they struggled to create a home [for me]."

The belief that they were to blame for their parents' struggles and therefore a burden not only influences people's identity, but it also seemed to motivate children of adolescent parents to behave in ways they believed would make their family members proud. The following section explores the connection between guilt, self-blame, and attributions of the burden on achievement-centered behavior in more detail.

Feeling Like There Is Something to Prove

Through the interviews, it became clear that those who felt guilty and believed they were a burden concluded that they had to take action to relieve themselves of their guilt. This atonement often took the form of seeking to achieve in order to prove their parents' struggles were not in vain. For example, Manuel reflected on how feeling like he was a burden meant he had to prove his worth. As he opened up about his reaction to his parents' struggles, he concluded,

But there was this, the second type of burden, which is that I felt like because I felt responsible for all this, I also felt like I had to succeed. I had to prove to them that I was worthwhile, even though . . . it would kill them to hear that.

Sarah (a 57-year-old Caucasian woman whose mother was 15 and father was 17 when she was born) made similar statements and said that hearing stories about the difficulties her parents experienced was particularly influential on her belief she had to prove her worth. When discussing how these stories influenced her, she concluded,

But the thing that I wrestled with that affected me my whole life and that I didn't realize it until . . . this therapist helped me see it . . . is that I, I guess I had to prove that it was okay that I was alive. Because I took responsibility for my parents having such difficult lives. And so, I had to make sure that it was okay that I was born.

Oftentimes, the enactment of this desire to prove one's worth was linked to academic achievement. For example, Kiana (a 19-year-old African American woman whose mother was 18 and father was 19 when she was born) reflected on how knowing her parents chose to keep her instead of putting her up for adoption was a motivating factor for her and her academic achievement. She said,

And so it pushes me more. It motivates me to wanna [*sic*] be better and wanna [*sic*] get my education and do everything that I can so I can give back. Give back to them and show them that those sacrifices were kinda [*sic*] worth it in a way.

Kiana's desire to prove her worth via her academic achievement sometimes added an additional burden to her life. For example, when discussing how difficult college was for her at the time of her interview, she mentioned that even though it was tough, she could not give up saying, "It's just kinda [*sic*] like, okay, I have to do this."

Another way the desire to prove their worth manifested in interviewees' lives involved making their family members proud. For example, when discussing her desire to always be her best, Ashley (a 37-year-old Caucasian woman whose mother was 16 and father was 20 when she was born) said,

I did feel like. . . . I had to do a good job. I felt like I had to prove to my maternal grandma that my parents made the right choice to marry and raise me together and I had to prove to my paternal grandparents that I wasn't going to make the same mistake as my parents because my parents were good parents that raised me right.

It is important to mention that the family stories Ashley highlighted in her interview included one focused on the fact that her maternal grandmother did not want her parents to get married and one focused on her paternal grandparents worry that she would become an adolescent parent as well. Based on her comment, clearly the stories she heard from both sides of her family left her feeling as if she had something to prove.

The need to prove their worth, particularly as this need relates to academic achievement, reflects perfectionism. In fact, when describing her desire to prove her worth, Erin used the term *perfection* specifically. She said,

> It's that sense of like, excellence, that you have to be excellent. A sense of perfection. I struggled with that for a while where everything had to be perfect. If it wasn't perfect, I failed. . . . I felt like perfection was a way to 'pay them back' for all they have done for me.

Interestingly, research has previously linked perfectionism to experiences with shame. Specifically, Sedighimornani, Rimes, and Verplanken (2020) found perfectionism can be a coping mechanism for shame. Although interviewees described experiencing guilt instead of shame, their sense of perfectionism may be a result of the shame their parents themselves may have felt due to their stigmatized status. Because those born to adolescent parents feel guilty about their parents' circumstances, they may also feel responsible for the shame their parents experience. Similar to feeling like their birth (and therefore they themselves) caused their parents' struggles, they may also feel like they were responsible for the shame their parents experienced because of being stigmatized; after all, their parents are stigmatized and shamed because of their birth. Therefore, to try to make up for the perceived responsibility for their parents' shame, they seek to appear perfect so that others approve of them, approve of their parents, and approve of their family despite their family's stigmatized form.

However, importantly, the desire to be perceived as perfect is an unattainable ideal. Thus, using perfectionism to seek to change how others see one's family can be futile. Perfectionism becomes a never-ending cycle whereby those born to adolescent parents are constantly trying to achieve more to prove their worth, but nothing they do is ever good enough because they can never actually be perfect or change the fact that their family form is stigmatized. This seeking of perfection and remarkable achievement can exacerbate the children's own identity issues. Now, not only do those born to adolescent parents feel like they must prove that they are worth their parents' struggles, but their inability to achieve perfection becomes more proof that they are not, in fact, "good enough."

This hamster wheel of seeking but never achieving perfection can become exhausting and demoralizing. In the interviews, many participants reflected on feeling as if they were constantly chasing something out of reach and discussed the harm it has caused their mental health. For example, Sarah mentioned how her self-blame and constant desire to prove her worth really hurt her view of herself and resulted in her seeking a therapist. Many interviewees spoke of going to therapy, engaging in extensive self-reflection, and/or using religion as ways to cope with and work through the blame they put on themselves as children. Based on the descriptions of interviewees, these types of coping mechanisms ultimately served to help the children of adolescent parents change their negative perceptions of their stories so that they could overcome their feelings of guilt and burden. The following chapter utilizes interview data to explain the process those born to adolescent parents enact in order to overcome this burden and guilt.

Chapter 4

Overcoming One's Burden

This chapter explores how those born to adolescent parents managed to overcome the burden and guilt associated with the birth, reproductive, or origin stories they were told throughout their lives. Like chapter 3, the information in this chapter is based specifically on discussions with interviewees, as the interviews provided the most descriptive information about the experiences of those born to adolescent parents. This chapter will therefore describe and present interview quotations to explore the processes interviewees reported going through in order to overcome feelings of guilt and burden described in chapter 3.

INTERPRETATIONS OF STORIES OVER TIME

One integral part of managing the feelings of burden and guilt interviewees mentioned experiencing was to alter how they understood and made sense of influential stories concerning their birth and/or their parents' lives that they have heard over time. To deal with these feelings, individuals must alter their understanding of such stories; therefore, before explaining the process individuals described going through to overcome their feelings of burden and guilt, it is first important to explain how interviewees altered their perceptions of influential stories over time. Although all interviewees mentioned experiencing a changed understanding of their story, regardless of whether the story provided *identity support* or led to an *identity struggle*, those who referenced stories associated with *identity struggle* were more likely to illustrate a transformation of understanding. Therefore, the examples provided within this section come from the interviews of those who described their stories as leading to an *identity struggle*.

One common change participants reported experiencing involved what was termed *acceptance*, which refers to a sense of understanding that one's parents did their best given their circumstances. Often this involved an interviewee developing a more positive outlook on the story they were told than the one they had developed when they were younger. Importantly, this theme of acceptance was specifically associated with how the interviewee viewed *their parents* and reflected their acceptance and understanding of who their parents were throughout their lives. Sometimes interviewees said because of their positive outlook, their most influential story became a motivator in their lives.

Emerson's (a 23-year-old Caucasian woman whose mother was 17 and father was 19 when she was born) experience provides a great example of someone whose understanding of their most influential story became more accepting over time. Emerson had a particularly difficult relationship with her mother due, in part, to her story. She noted,

> So in some ways I don't look on my past with as much resentment and anger as I did, especially in high school and then into very early adulthood. And so, I don't blame my parents as much for my experiences. I kinda [*sic*] wish that they had been different, but I understand that my parents are who they are, and my experiences were what they were. All I can do is just learn from them and just look ahead.

Manuel (a 35-year-old Hispanic male whose parents were both 17 when he was born) echoed this idea of accepting and understanding his parents as they are or were. When reflecting on how his interpretation of his most influential story has changed over time, he said,

> That's why I said I think a lot of this was things beyond my parents' control . . . when you think about being a teenager, being a parent and the fact that we're all alive and all of us are successful in our ways . . . hey, kudos to them.

In this quote Manuel describes how over time he was able to perceive that his parents did the best they could and that everything turned out okay, thus accepting his parents and their life circumstances.

Naomi's (a 24-year-old African American woman whose mother was 18 and father was 19 when she was born) description of how her understanding of her most influential story has changed provides a good example of how a more positive association with one's most influential story can also be used as motivation in one's life. Naomi reported,

> So I think after a while, I did turn it into motivation. I think it also just gave me an even bigger appreciation of my mom and stuff. Just that she had to change

her plans kind of abruptly, and yet she's still a great person . . . she always told us she didn't want us to be like her, and I'm like, "Well, I actually want to be like you."

For Naomi, once she accepted her parents' humanness, she was able to use that new understanding to push her to work hard (while discussing her motivation Naomi was discussing her academic pursuits). Perhaps the most important part of Naomi's quote is that because of her acceptance of her mother, she identified wanting to be like her mother. This completely pushes against the stigmatization of adolescent parenthood, which suggests being like one's adolescent parent leads to failure. Naomi has turned that belief on its head by saying her mother is a great person regardless of how young she was when Naomi was born, and because of that, she hopes she *can* be like her mom.

In all these preceding examples related to the theme of *acceptance*, those born to adolescent parents were able to reflect on their childhood experiences and the negative influence their stories have had on their identity and realize that their parents did everything they could to give them good lives. Each person who went through this process also referenced that they now understand they cannot blame their parents for how their own lives turned out; instead, they must accept the past and move forward with a more positive outlook.

Another common change interviewees outlined was termed *agency*, which involves taking control of one's story and letting go of the blame they took on as children. Importantly, while the *acceptance* theme focused on accepting their parents' limitations and circumstances, the theme of *agency* focused on respondents' own role in their story and the realization that they cannot harbor guilt for choices they themselves did not make. This theme of *agency* is particularly important when considering the implications of stories associated with *identity struggle*. By taking agency of their own story, those born to adolescent parents shed self-blame and become free from their perceived burden and guilt. For example, when discussing how his understanding of his story has changed over time, Manuel stated,

> When I was young, I couldn't help but take [the stories] personally. It was hard not to think that you're an accident, you're a mistake, that you impacted your parents' life in ways that they regret. But I think somehow [in graduate school] my understanding changed.

When interpreting this quote, it is important to remember that earlier in the interview, Manuel talked a lot about how he blamed himself for his parents' circumstances (see chapter 3). Therefore, when he talks about taking responsibility, he is referring to the blame he took on and says eventually his understanding of who was to blame (so to speak) or who had the ultimate

responsibility for his family's situation changed. Manuel's change in understanding of who was to "blame" is what makes this aspect of Manuel's
change in interpretation of the story about *agency*.

Sarah (a 57-year-old Caucasian woman whose mother was 15 and father
was 17 when she was born) made similar comments related to self-agency
when discussing the importance of therapy in her life. Therapy has given her
tools to use when she starts to blame herself for her parents' circumstances.
Sarah explained,

> Sometimes I might have a reaction, but I can, I know where it came from. I can
> understand it and so then I can defuse it. If it's a positive [thought] that's great,
> I can continue . . . but if it's a negative [thought] I [can diffuse it] . . . we all
> have value. We don't need to prove anything. Or justify our existence. We are
> all valuable. And we're all here; there's something that we're all learning that's
> going to contribute to the bigger picture.

In this example, Sarah was talking about her tendency to blame herself, and
how by applying tools from therapy she has learned to stop herself from
believing those thoughts when they arise and remember that she has value
without needing to prove her worth—that she has nothing to feel guilty about.

The connection between the change in understanding associated with
acceptance and *agency* and managing blame and guilt can be extrapolated
by research on how people cope with trauma and stress. Joseph and Linley
(2008) used the term *posttraumatic growth* to refer to a process of adjustment
that engenders new positive appraisals of past events. In their description of
this process, they specify that instead of focusing on improving subjective
well-being (defined as seeking to achieve happiness and avoid pain) following adversity, posttraumatic growth is about improving psychological
well-being. The idea of posttraumatic growth is particularly relevant to the
interviewees' experiences because it illuminates how participants coped with
any guilt or stress associated with witnessing their parents' struggle. More
specifically, the idea of posttraumatic growth highlights why it is so important that the interviewees alter the understanding of their stories and think of
their life experiences more positively.

Joseph and Linley (2008) explain that there are three dimensions of posttraumatic growth: (1) changes in life philosophy, which relate to developing
autonomy and finding purpose in one's life; (2) changes in perceptions of
self, which relate to environmental mastery, successfully managing environmental factors, and taking advantage of opportunities, personal growth, and
self-acceptance; and (3) changes in relationships with others, which relate
to developing positive relationships with other people. The idea of *acceptance* identified in interviewees' experiences relates specifically to *positive
relationships with others*, as acceptance involves altering the perceptions of

one's parents so that they are viewed more positively. Additionally, the idea of *agency* involves both *changes in life philosophy* and *changes in percep-tions of self*, as the theme of *agency* relates to developing autonomy over one's story and realizing one is not responsible for their parents' choices.

Overall, by applying Joseph and Linley's (2008) concept of posttraumatic growth to the experiences of interviewees, it becomes clear that changing the way they think about their life circumstances and their interpretation of the most influential stories they were told as children is absolutely central to man-aging the harmful influence of stories those born to adolescent parents inter-preted negatively as children. It is through these changes, especially taking agency over their lives, that interviewees were able to transform their thought processes resulting in a healthier self-concept. In this case, the change was specifically being able to move on from the guilt and burden they placed on themselves as children. The process of change that has been previewed here will be discussed in more detail in the next section, which delineates the main theoretical contribution provided by this book in terms of understanding chil-dren of adolescent parents: the *agency-driven attribution shift*.

Agency-Driven Attribution Shift

The *agency-driven attribution shift* process is a term developed by the first author that utilizes information discussed in earlier chapters to identify what steps those born to adolescent parents have taken to try to work through the identity-related issues caused by the combination of witnessing their parents' struggle, experiencing stigmatization, and hearing stories associated with identity struggle. The *agency-driven attribution shift* process involves (1) taking agency over one's story, which entails realizing that their childhood interpretations of certain family stories were not accurate and can be changed, and (2) shifting the attributions they made for their parents' struggles as children, which includes realizing *they* were not to blame for their parents' choices. When these two processes occur, it results in a more positive inter-pretation of their story and life circumstances. Given that this process outlines moving from a negative interpretation of one's story and dealing with guilt and feeling like a burden, the *agency-driven attribution shift* process applies only to those born to adolescent parents who have negative experiences in the first place. Those who went through this process (1) witnessed their parents' struggling, (2) blamed themselves for that struggle, and (3) used their child-hood interpretation of stories they were told by family members to support their feelings of guilt and self-blame.

Consequently, the *agency-driven attribution shift* developed because chil-dren of adolescent parents were experiencing a type of identity crisis, and they realized that they needed to alter the negative way in which they interpreted their life circumstances. As stated earlier, for many children of adolescent parents, this process involved working with a therapist to help themselves realize they should not be blamed for their parents' choices. Another common avenue to jumpstart the agency-driven attribution shift involved engaging in an introspective process to realize that they internalized blame for something over which they had no control, their own birth.

Although the identity crisis described earlier seemed to be what sparks the beginning of the *agency-driven attribution shift* process in the interviewees, the actual act of ridding oneself of blame occurred as a result of *taking agency over the stories they were told*, which required people to *purposefully change the attributions they made as a child*. By both taking agency of their story and changing their childhood attributions, those born to adolescent parents were able to realize that their *thoughts* were the issue and not their *existence*. This realization seemed to spark the shift in perspective many individuals experienced, although this shift likely was not easy, nor did it seem to happen immediately. The steps associated with this attribution shift are more fully described next.

Altering one's childhood attributions about their families' experiences was the first step in the *agency-driven attribution shift* process. Those born to adolescent parents were only able to cast away their guilt, sense of burden, and desire to prove their worth when they could reject the idea that they were responsible for their parents' choices and place the locus of control for their parents' struggles outside of themselves (i.e., when they altered the attributions they originally made for their parents/family struggles). According to Koenig Kellas and Kranstuber Horstman's (2015) Communicated Narrative Sensemaking theory, the process of making attributions is central to the sensemaking process; therefore, it is not surprising that interviewees who went through the *agency-driven attribution shift* recognized that, on some level, the attributions they made as children were faulty and harmful.

Changing the locus of control from internal (it is their fault that their parents struggled due to their birth) to external (they cannot take responsibility for their parents' choices) required participants to focus on the positive aspects of their life and *take agency* over how they interpreted and the stories they were told. Taking agency of one's story is thus the second step in the agency-driven attribution shift process. Taking agency involved realizing that those born to adolescent parents could control how they interpreted the stories they were told; they did not have to be held captive to the version of the story they told themselves as young children. During this process, interviewees allowed themselves simultaneously to acknowledge that their birth was an event that caused their parents to struggle, but that their birth was not *their* fault. In essence, interviewees were able to realize that because they could not foresee that their own birth would cause their parents to struggle and because they had no control over their birth in the first place, the stories they were told were not further proof that they were "bad" and needed to prove their worth; they realized they must let go of this burden.

Importantly, based on the description of many interviewees, nothing their parents told them helped them overcome the damage that watching their parents struggle had on their identity. Instead, they had to go through this internal thought process that allowed them to shift responsibility for the struggles their families experienced from themselves (due to their birth) to their parents' own choices, and they had to realize that their parents did the best they could given their circumstances, instead of harboring resentment against them. To rid oneself of guilt and burden associated with being born to adolescent parents, interviewees had to formulate a different perspective of their story, and essentially rewrite their interpretation of it, which is why the change in perspective discussed earlier in the chapter is so essential. The shift in how individuals thought about their story and their ability to rewrite their story as adults seem to represent a fundamental change in their *personal myth*, as McAdams (1993) describes the concept.

Do All Children of Adolescent Parents Experience the Agency-Driven Attribution Shift?

It is important to note that there were two interviewees (out of eight) whose experiences did not follow the full pattern described by the *agency-driven attribution shift*. The circumstances surrounding their experiences can be useful as a negative case analysis, which occurs when researchers can use cases that do not fit their data's overall pattern to further explicate and develop their overall conclusions (Bisel and Barge 2011). Next, there are details about the two interviewees who did not experience the *agency-driven attribution shift*, along with details from their life experience to explain why it makes sense that they did not—ultimately providing support for the overall process described in the *agency-driven attribution shift* for those who did experience it.

The first individual whose experiences did not completely align with *agency-driven attribution shift* was Emerson (a 23-year-old Caucasian woman whose mother was 17 and father was 19 when she was born). Emerson watched her family struggle, and she described her childhood as tumultuous. Her relationship with her mother has been strained, and part of that strain was due to a story her mother told her that insisted that her birth gave her mother's life purpose. Despite a story that sounds positive on the surface, Emerson consistently said that the story became a source of pressure for her, and the idea that she was her mother's purpose became a burden. She believed that her mother had no identity outside of her children and that her relationship with her mother became very "co-dependent," which ended up resulting in Emerson deciding she did not want to be anything like her mother. Emerson noted that she experienced stress as a child. She felt a sense of burden and moved through that burden by realizing her mother's issues are her own and not something she can control; however, Emerson never experienced issues associated with guilt, nor the need to prove that her existence was worth the struggles her family went through, aspects of the *agency-driven attribution shift* other individuals born to adolescent parents in the study experienced.

Based on Emerson's description of her life, it makes sense theoretically that she never needed to prove her worth because the entire point of her mother's story was that Emerson's existence was more than enough; in fact, it was everything. Emerson's sense of burden came from the fact that her mother placed responsibility for her own happiness on Emerson's shoulders, not from taking personal responsibility for her mother's choices after watching her struggle. While Emerson went through some of the experiences associated with *agency-driven attribution shift*, the essence of her story and the way it influenced her meant guilt about her birth and proving her worth were never part of her personal identity struggle. Therefore, it was not Emerson's *attributions* about her parents' struggles that caused issues for her; instead, it was her mother's reliance on her that was so damaging.

The other person whose experience did not match the process described by the concept of *agency-driven attribution shift* was Rebecca. Although Rebecca (a 47-year-old Caucasian woman whose parents were both 19 when she was born) experienced some struggles growing up, she described her most influential story, that her parents got pregnant with her on purpose so they could get married, as a positive and funny one, and said she never experienced feelings of guilt or that she was a burden. An examination of two struggles Rebecca described during her interview helps explain why she did not go through the *agency-driven attribution shift*. One struggle involved her paternal grandmother initially disapproving of her parents' relationship because her parents were so young and her mother was from a "not very good family." Her grandmother's disapproval strained the relationship between her mother and her paternal grandmother when Rebecca was very young, but this strained relationship improved when Rebecca was still a child, and their relationship has been positive for most of her life. The second struggle occurred when her elementary school principal questioned her parents' choices for her education, and mentioned wondering how Rebecca was so smart, essentially suggesting (1) her parents were not capable of making the right choices due to their age and (2) because her parents were young, it was remarkable that Rebecca did so well in school.

While these two situations could have caused identity-related issues for someone else, Rebecca described these negative experiences as unfortunate, but as having no negative influence on her. The reason why Rebecca's paternal grandmother's disapproval of her parents' relationship did not have a negative influence on her is because her mother and paternal grandmother resolved this issue. Rebecca also mentioned that the original disapproval was not an ongoing issue because she understands that her grandmother was worried getting married so young would keep her father from going to college and having a good job. Importantly, Rebecca is the only interviewee whose father earned a graduate degree. Her mother earned her high school degree before she was born, her father completed a master's degree while she was growing up, and at the time of her interview, he had a PhD. At the end of the day, her grandmother's fears were unfounded. She also described her father as being in the oil business, and her parents have remained married for her entire life. She never described any relationship issues between them that she witnessed. Instead, she described her parents and herself as a happy three-person unit who have always been close.

Her father's education was also a reason why her experience with her elementary school principal did not seem to affect her identity negatively. When the principal questioned her parents' ability to make good decisions for Rebecca, her father mentioned his graduate degrees to prove he could make choices for his daughter even though he was young when she was born. She also said that while her principal's comments about her academic ability were inappropriate, as a child she was mostly confused by them and simply did not understand why her parents' age should have any influence on her own ability. Even as a child, she did not internalize the stigmatizing statements she encountered, and this could relate to the success of her parents and the supportive atmosphere she grew up within. Overall, although Rebecca witnessed a few struggles her family went through, she never perceived that there was any reason to blame herself for anything negative that she described. Her parents were successful, and even her paternal grandmother's fear that her father would not go to college was not realized.

The stories Rebecca heard also never made her question her value. There was no reason for Rebecca to blame herself for anything or to feel guilty because her existence gave her parents everything they ever wanted, and they were always a happy, highly functional family unit. She did mention having a sense of acceptance when thinking back on her story, but this acceptance was not about accepting that she was not to blame for her parents' choices. Instead, this acceptance focused on realizing that her grandmother only wanted what was best for her father even though she originally did not support Rebecca's parents' choices. Rebecca perceived herself as wanted, planned for, and highly desired. Her birth was the final piece of the puzzle that her parents so desperately wanted in their lives. Rebecca had no *agency-driven attribution shift* to go through because she never took responsibility for her parents' struggles in the first place.

Overall, although Emerson and Rebecca did not go through the *agency-driven attribution shift*, a look at their individual circumstances illustrates potential reasons why they did not go through the full process. Therefore, as Bisel and Barge (2011) suggested, the negative case analysis involving Emerson and Rebecca's situations provides further evidence to support the key elements of the *agency-driven attribution shift* described in this chapter. First, prior to the shift, those born to adolescent parents must witness their family struggle in some way. They must blame themselves for that struggle, resulting in guilt about their family's circumstances. Lastly, their self-blame and guilt must become a filter that influences how they interpret the stories they are told as children, ultimately meaning the stories they are told reinforce their sense of burden and guilt. When these three situations exist, the *agency-driven attribution shift* process can occur as long as those born to adolescent parents do the work to alter their understanding of their life circumstances, including their understanding of their parents, in a more positive direction *and* realize they are not actually to blame for their own existence.

The next and final chapter summarizes the information provided in the first four chapters of this book and goes into more depth concerning how various family circumstances, such as education of one's parents, education of those born to adolescent parents themselves, social support of extended family networks, and the overall sense of connection among family members, influence whether someone born to adolescent parents progresses through the *agency-driven attribution shift*. The last chapter also provides practical advice to researchers, practitioners, and family members of those born to adolescent parents.

Chapter 5

Conclusions

The study described in this book set out to understand whether those born to adolescent parents experienced stigma because of their family form, as well as whether storytelling was an influential communication process in their families. The overarching goal was to see how both stigma and storytelling, both individually and together, influenced the identity of those born to adolescent parents. The conclusions described in the preceding chapters have provided invaluable insight into these processes. The aim of this final chapter is to reflect on everything described previously in an effort to synthesize information, as well as to utilize the research findings to provide some practical advice for those from families with adolescent parents, as well as practitioners and researchers.

The overarching takeaway is that stigmatization of adolescent parents and family storytelling often works together to influence how those born to adolescent parents view themselves and engage in sensemaking concerning their family's circumstances. Importantly, to fully understand how and why stigmatization and storytelling have this influence, one must consider the experiences of each individual's unique family, including any struggles they might have gone through and the type of support system(s) they have been able to rely on. Additionally, it is necessary to consider the ways in which those born to adolescent parents *interpret* family stories about their births and origins, not necessarily the *intent* of their family members when telling the story. For better or for worse, their family experiences act as a filter, influencing how those born to adolescent parents make sense of the stories they are told as children. The good news is that, despite how negatively someone might interpret the stories they are told, and therefore how negatively their interpretation of those stories might influence how they view themselves, it is possible for those born to adolescent parents to alter this negative sense of self. The following section expands upon these conclusions and provides advice for families of adolescent parents, practitioners, and scholars.

BRINGING IT ALL TOGETHER

The Influence of the Stigmatization of Adolescent Parenthood

Both survey data and the interview findings from the study highlighted in this book provide insight into the first main conclusion the authors would like to focus on: the way stigmatization influences those born to adolescent parents. As outlined in chapter 1, although society does not currently have as intense a focus on the "problem" of adolescent pregnancy as it did in the 1980s and 1990s, members of families of adolescent parents still report experiencing stigmatization. Importantly, study data suggest children of adolescent parents are aware of their parents' stigmatized status, which shows they recognize how others view their parents, and the children consider this stigmatized view as an extension of themselves and their families more broadly.

Unfortunately, survey data also show that negative views of adolescent parenthood in general can still cause harm even if one's family members do not actually experience stigmatization directly. Survey participants indicated that the more their parents simply worried about being stigmatized, the more the participants were likely to worry about being stigmatized themselves, even after controlling for a variety of influential factors such as demographic information and characteristics of their family relationships. The overall lesson here is that when members of society, or even societal systems like governments, condemn adolescent parenthood, the impact of that condemnation for at least some children of adolescent parents is that they believe their parents are "bad" and they worry they are perceived as "bad" too. In fact, survey data also illustrated that when people perceived their parents as stigmatized, their self-esteem was lower than those who did not perceive their parents as stigmatized. Again, this relationship remained even after controlling for other demographic and relational factors.

Not only are those born to adolescent parents aware of and influenced by their parents' stigmatization (real or perceived), that stigmatization becomes a filter through which they see the world. For example, experiences with stigmatization represent one type of struggle families may experience that those born to adolescent parents then blame themselves for. As many interviewees noted, as children they concluded that they were to blame for their parents' experiences. This internalized blame then colored how those born to adolescent parents interpreted the stories they were told as young children.

This finding does not suggest that society necessarily needs to encourage adolescent parenthood or glamorize it anyway. Being an adolescent parent is hard, and research has repeatedly shown having children as an adolescent has a negative influence on one's life outcomes. For example, statistics from the National Campaign to Prevent Teen Pregnancy (cited by the National Conference of State Legislatures 2013) show that less than 2% of adolescent mothers obtain a college degree by age 30, and only 51% graduate high school compared to 89% of those who do not give birth as an adolescent. About 30% of those who drop out of high school indicate their decision was influenced by pregnancy and/or parenthood (National Conference of State Legislatures 2013). Certainly, this influence of pregnancy on graduation rates and college attendance also negatively influences future economic earnings and stability. Adolescent parents are also more likely to experience relationship instability, with results of the National Survey of Family Growth showing that 9% of adolescent mothers are married by the time their child turns three (Manning and Cohen 2015). Despite these hardships, concerns about negative outcomes associated with adolescent parenthood should be communicated to adolescent parents and their family members in a way that does not stigmatize these family members and cause harm. Furthermore, it is also important to remember that not all aspects of the lives of adolescent parents and their children are negative. As described in chapter 1, focusing on only negative outcomes perpetuates the stigmatization of adolescent parenthood and can have unintended consequences (Smithbattle 2013), including adolescent parents feeling like their lives are constantly under surveillance, and reporting harmful encounters with healthcare providers (Brand, Morrison, and Down 2014).

While stigmatization was one type of struggle that influenced how those born to adolescent parents interpreted stories they were told about their existence, other struggles—such as relationship problems and economic hardship—were also factors many interviewees mentioned as being influential. These struggles were physically verifiable and not necessarily based on how others stigmatized them. However, before writing these experiences off as unrelated to stigma, one must wonder whether those born to adolescent parents would have been as likely to blame themselves for those circumstances were the dominant narrative about adolescent parenthood not so negative and focused on detrimental life outcomes. If society did not clearly communicate that having a baby early will doom a family to economic hardship, would children be less likely to blame themselves for their parents' economic struggles? It is impossible to answer these questions clearly because of the overlapping nature between stigmatization of adolescent parenthood and various struggles families of adolescent parents face. However, based on how interviewees talked about their experiences, one can surmise that it is somewhat likely that stigmatization of adolescent parenthood encouraged those born to adolescent parents to see themselves as the source of their parents' struggles and generally negative status in society.

Overall, being an adolescent parent is hard work, and there is not necessarily anything wrong with admitting that reality. Such perceptions become problematic when, as individuals and as a society, people focus on that hardship and begin shaming adolescent parents, or even the idea of adolescent parenthood: when people begin making adolescent parents feel like they are unworthy, that they harm society, and that they are destined for failure, in other words when they are stigmatized. Those messages do not help anyone, least of all the children of adolescent parents who never asked to be born but still wade into the pool of society's judgment daily. Everyone, then, can benefit by being more aware of how they talk about adolescent parenthood, and everyone should consider the unintended consequences of their words, as well as policy decisions based on those words.

Instead of judgment, the data show that society should focus on ensuring adolescent parents have adequate support systems, as support was integral for the positive adjustment of those born to adolescent parents who participated in this project. For example, people with close-knit families were less likely to be negatively impacted by stigmatization, which was reflected in Rebecca's (a 47-year-old Caucasian woman whose parents were both 19 when she was born) experience. Rebecca watched her parents be stigmatized in her presence during a meeting with a principal but replied this incident did not negatively influence her partially because she and her family were such a supportive, close group. The importance of support will be further discussed in the section on practical advice.

The Importance of Storytelling

Above and beyond the important ways stigmatization influences the lives of those born to adolescent parents, the second main conclusion from this research is that storytelling was an important communication strategy used in families of adolescent parents and that stories themselves had an influence on the identity of those born to adolescent parents. Results of both survey data and the interview findings support the importance of storytelling, particularly stories concerning the child's birth, conception, or existence. Additionally, almost 70% of those born to adolescent parents reported hearing a story about their birth, conception, or existence from their family. Thus, as in all families, storytelling is ubiquitous among families with adolescent parents.

Additionally, survey results provided insight as to *why* storytelling is so prominent. Galvin's (2006) categorization of storytelling as an important family communication tactic used by members of discourse-dependent families suggests storytelling could be used in response to stigmatization as a way for family members to protect their children from the negative implications of being stigmatized. In this way, the intent of storytelling for these family members would be to rewrite the way people talk about adolescent parenthood—to show children that they are not destined for failure just because their parent(s) was(were) young when they were born. Again, both survey data and interview findings in this study supported this idea. Results of the survey showed parental stigmatization significantly predicted the use of storytelling as a communication tactic in families, and interviews garnered specific examples of stories people were told in response to societal stigmatization. For example, Sarah's (a 57-year-old Caucasian woman whose mother was 15 and father was 17 when she was born) mom told her she could achieve great things, and Kiana's (a 19-year-old African American woman whose mother was 18 and father was 19 when she was born) and Erin's (a 22-year-old Caucasian female whose mother was 18 and father was 19 when she was born) mothers told them they were not mistakes. Each of these stories directly reflects common negative societal beliefs about children of adolescent parents and serves to let the child know that the negative societal belief does not apply to them.

The connection between stigma and storytelling is complicated and seemingly reciprocal given that stories are told in response to or in defense against stigmatization, but it is clear that real or perceived stigmatization influences how someone interprets the family stories they are told. Unfortunately, this reciprocal relationship also means that the positive intentions of family members do not always match the impact the stories have on the children themselves, muddying the connection between storytelling and identity. To illustrate the mismatch between family intent and impact on the child, there were two specific interviewees who wrote about stories that seem positive to an objective individual and that they believe were told to them with positive intentions, but that they perceived in a negative manner, and that, in turn, negatively influenced their identity. Emerson's (a 23-year-old Caucasian female whose mother was 17 and father was 19 when she was born) story focused on how her birth gave her mother purpose and saved her from what her mother believed could have been a downward spiral had Emerson not been born. To outside listeners, hearing that their birth had such a positive influence on their parent's life might seem positive and uplifting, but for Emerson, this story became a burden that negatively influenced her relationship with her mother for years.

Additionally, Erin mentioned that her mother would tell her that she was chosen and that her parents wanted her to be in their lives. Again, this story sounds as if it has a positive tone, but Erin had also heard contradictory stories from other family members. Because of the mismatch in the information provided in both versions of her birth/reproductive/origin story, she felt her mother's story was a lie. Even though she believes her mother had good intentions in telling her the story, she said the story negatively influenced her self-esteem. This low self-esteem is something with which she has dealt throughout her adult life, at least so far. One way Erin has sought to deal with this self-esteem issue includes discussing the story with a therapist who helped her work through the influence it has had on her identity. Both Emerson and Erin's experiences highlight how stories with a positive intent do not always have a positive influence on those born to adolescent parents.

The idea of *agency-driven attribution shift* can help explain why the intent family members have when telling a story may not be particularly influential to the identity development in children of adolescent parents. Recall that the *agency-driven attribution shift* process suggested that nothing their parents told those born to adolescent parents helped change their negative interpretation of the stories they were told. The only factor that helped was the internal process of realizing they, the children, were not to blame for their parents' circumstances and letting go of any guilt they might still have about their parents' circumstances. Therefore, according to the *agency-driven attribution shift*, no story family members tell those born to adolescent parents is guaranteed to help the children see their existence in a positive light. Instead, it is most important to consider attribution processes children go through about their parents' experiences. The importance of being aware of the attributions children of adolescent parents make is discussed further in the practical applications section of this chapter.

Relatedly, conclusions outlined in this book, particularly related to interview findings, also illustrate how important it was to examine the influence of family storytelling in tandem with stigma. Take Ashley (a 37-year-old Caucasian female whose mother was 16 and father was 20 when she was born) as an example. As she described her experiences with stigmatization, Ashley mentioned that while she was growing up, her father's family made negative comments about her mother's status as an adolescent parent. Ashley also mentioned that her grandmother would tell her stories about how hard her mother's life was, and as Ashley heard these stories, she internalized the blame for her mother's struggles and believed it was her fault that her mother did not reach her potential. She specifically mentioned feeling like she was a burden to her. This example highlights the connections between stigma, storytelling, and internalizing blame. Ashley's own family made stigmatizing comments about her mother, the stories she was told by her grandmother supported the stigmatization of adolescent parenthood, and combined, the stigma she witnessed and stories she was told led to her feeling guilty for keeping her parents from meeting their potential. Notably, Ashley also went through the *agency-driven attribution shift* after she realized that she had no control over her birth and/or her parents' life outcomes. According to Ashley, going through this process allowed her to think more positively about her life, as well as her parents' lives, and has kept her from continuing to think of herself as a burden. Now, she says, she reflects on everything in her and her parents' lives and realized "god had a plan" all along and everything that happened to her and her family was part of that plan.

HOW FAMILY RELATIONAL FACTORS AND ECONOMIC CONCERNS INFLUENCE THE RELATIONSHIP BETWEEN STIGMA, STORYTELLING, AND IDENTITY

Prior to moving on to practical advice, it is important to highlight the importance of two factors that impact how stigmatization and storytelling influence children's identities: (1) family relational factors and (2) economic concerns. Results of analyses of the survey data showed family cohesion, family closeness, and participant education were influential covariates[1] in many analyses. In fact, before these variables were considered, the observed relationship between personal experiences with stigmatization predicted participant self-esteem, and the tone (positive or negative) of a story research participants identified as influential predicted one's self-esteem, but after family cohesion, family closeness, and participant education were added to analyses, these two relationships became nonsignificant. Therefore, it is important to consider why family cohesion, family closeness, and participant education would alter outcomes within families with adolescent parents.

Regarding stigma, those individuals who came from cohesive and close family units were potentially able to work together to overcome the stigma those born to adolescent parents experienced. For example, they could use their family members as a support system for managing the stigma, and their familial support could help them reject this stigma instead of internalizing it (Meisenbach 2010). Joseph and Linley (2008) specifically mention that supportive environments are important for helping people positively cope with stressful events, providing even more compelling evidence that family support is integral to the process of protecting the self-esteem of those born to adolescent parents.

Familial support also might explain why perceived positivity or negativity of an influential story one was told did not significantly predict self-esteem once family cohesion and family closeness were added to the analysis. Results from the interviews can illustrate why support was so influential. For example, one of the themes that emerged from the interview data was that many of those born to adolescent parents described their family environment as supportive and close, and discussed how important familial support was to their success. Even those who did go through identity struggles related to the most influential stories they were told seemed to reference their family's support as helping them remain positive in the face of adversity, and perhaps helping them move through the *agency-driven attribution shift*. For example, when describing how her understanding of her most influential story has changed over time Naomi (a 24-year-old African American female whose mother was 18 and father was 19 when she was born) talked about how her appreciation of her mother helped keep her motivated and on track academically. She talked about how her mother was always there for her and her siblings and how she hoped to be like her mom someday. It was clear from her interview responses that the support Naomi felt from her mother throughout her life helped her have a positive outlook on her life.

Additionally, the variable of *participant education* may be influential because more education led to a higher ability to reject their stigma instead of internalizing it. This possibility of the protective value of education is supported by the interview findings. For example, when describing the shift in their thought patterns so that they no longer blamed themselves for their parents' choices, many interviewees pointed to the idea that as they got older and learned more, they realized that blaming themselves for situations out of their control was pointless. In fact, Manuel (a 35-year-old Hispanic male whose parents were both 17 when he was born) mentioned that his thought process about his life experiences began to change while he was studying for his PhD. Other individuals born to adolescent parents also mentioned that as they received tangible evidence of their academic ability (e.g., receiving high grades), they realized that other people's views of what they were capable of were not accurate. For example, Sarah described having this experience in her interview. After reading an article that suggested those born to adolescent parents were destined to be uneducated and poor, Sarah's mother and grandmother made sure to tell her that she was smart and capable. Sarah also mentioned that she was able to believe her mother and grandmother's words only because she also received good grades in school. The external evidence of Sarah's academic achievements worked to disprove the idea that she was destined for failure, which ultimately helped her reject the stigma of adolescent parenthood. Lastly, participant educational achievement may help explain why tone of the story no longer predicted self-esteem once participant education was considered. Essentially, one's own educational achievement can illustrate to those born to adolescent parents that they are capable and smart, making the tone of the stories they are told as children about their families less relevant to how they viewed themselves.

Overall, the big picture painted by the survey results and the interview findings suggests that witnessing some sort of family struggle (which is a family situation often brought on by demographic and family characteristics) is at the heart of the identity-related issues those born to adolescent parents experience. This family struggle is linked to instances of stigmatization that occurred because one's parent was an adolescent when they were born, and at times the experience of stigma itself becomes a struggle that those born to adolescent parents witnessed. Witnessing one's parents struggle also can lead to an internalized sense of responsibility for the issues those born to adolescent parents saw their families experience, which then resulted in feelings of guilt, believing one is a burden to one's family, and feeling the need to prove the worthiness of one's existence. For those whose families were close and supportive or those that were highly educated or experienced high personal academic achievement, some of these negative implications could be avoided or rectified over time. In essence, issues brought on by socioeconomic status and family relationship struggles were potential external catalysts for the experiences that negatively influenced the identity of those born to adolescent parents and ultimately led to the necessity of, and experience with, the *agency-driven attribution shift* later in one's life for these individuals. Members of families of adolescent parents who would like to remedy these potential identity issues in their children can seek to increase the likelihood of doing so by creating close, supportive family environments and highlighting the academic achievements of those born to adolescent parents. The following section provides more details about what family members can do to help those born to adolescent parents manage or avoid negative identity concerns.

WHAT NOW? PRACTICAL IMPLICATIONS FOR FAMILIES AND PRACTITIONERS AND IDEAS FOR RESEARCHERS

While the conclusions drawn from this study provide important theoretical insights, to maximize the potential impact of the ideas discussed here, it is useful to consider how these findings relate to practical advice and/or guidance to others. In this section, practical implications for families and practitioners are advanced, as well as ideas researchers interested in either communication within families of adolescent parents or the influence of family stories should consider as they engage in related scholarship.

Advice for Families

Given the importance of social support to the outcomes children of adolescent parents experience, and the way support influenced the relationships examined in this project in particular, one action families of adolescent parents can integrate into their routine is to work to ensure their children are brought up in a supportive atmosphere. For a few of the interviewees, the support they received from family members either made it easier for them to let go of damaging thought patterns that resulted from stigmatization as they went through the *agency-driven attribution shift* later in life, or the support helped them to avoid negative implications of stigmatization all together, rendering the *agency-driven attribution shift* unnecessary. Adolescent parents, as well as other family members in general, should not only speak to their children in a supportive manner but *specifically and clearly* remind them that they are not a mistake, and not destined for failure.

Additionally, the importance of supportive communication and the influence this type of communication had on some interviewees' ability to let go of negative thoughts each suggest parents should talk to their children specifically about the idea of self-blame. None of the interviewees mentioned talking to their parents about the feeling of responsibility they developed for their parents' circumstances as children. In fact, many interviewees said that if their parents knew they felt as if they were a burden, their parents would be extremely upset. In many circumstances, parents seemed to openly communicate with their children about their academic abilities and/or the idea that they were chosen (i.e., not a mistake), but it does not seem that parents even realized their children felt guilty or felt as if they were a burden. Perhaps if adolescent parents brought up the idea of self-blame during conversations with their children in a supportive way, they could help their children reverse any negative thought patterns before self-blame can severely harm their identity. If nothing else, engaging in a supportive conversation about childhood self-blame might help those born to adolescent parents work through their issues and concerns earlier than they would have if they kept their burden to themselves. Therefore, adolescent parents specifically, and their family networks more generally, should try to identify behaviors that suggest their children are trying to prove their worth (such as being unusually self-motivated and/or taking care of oneself as a child), and have conversations about self-blame with their children.

The results of the study outlined in this book also highlight the importance of being an effective storyteller if adolescent parents want to help their children manage their experiences with stigma. Notably, some parents were able to tell stories that children perceived positively, and therefore these adolescent parents or family members mitigated the negative outcomes associated with stigma, such as those stories told by Rebecca's parents, and some stories told by both Kiana's (a 19-year-old African American woman whose mother was 18 and father was 19 when she was born) and Naomi's (a 24-year-old African American woman whose mother was 18 and father was 19 when she was born) mothers. In a practical sense, this suggests some parents may be more effective than others at telling stories that discourage the internalization of blame and stigma. Many of the results highlighted here focused on the role and actions that children of adolescent parents took in order to move past their childhood attributions of blame or guilt, but there is also an opportunity for parents to use storytelling as a chance to take agency of their life choices and the influences of these life choices on their children.

The most important takeaway when it comes to effective storytelling involves understanding the impact of one's words when telling a family story. For example, given that it was the participants' *perception* of the tone of stories told to them that related to their likelihood of engaging in self-blame, parents should not only consider whether they believe they are telling positive stories but also how their children might interpret the stories they tell. Thus, adolescent parents should seek to clarify the interpretation of the stories they tell, and openly talk to their children about how they are interpreting their family stories.

Advice for Practitioners

It is also important to consider how practitioners can utilize the insights from this book to help families of adolescent parents. While there is no "one size fits all" way to help families with adolescent parents, conclusions highlighted here do provide some jumping-off points that practitioners, such as therapists or support group leaders, could use to help families maintain healthy relationships and avoid some of the negative outcomes associated with adolescent parenthood. Many of the practical implications for families discussed previously provide insight into areas where practitioners could provide help and suggestions. For example, practitioners could work with families to develop a supportive atmosphere for both the adolescent parents themselves and their children. This might involve family therapy or encouraging members of the family to seek outside support if their family members cannot or will not be there for them.

Additionally, it is important that members of families with adolescent parents develop strong observation and listening skills. For example, because it is important that parents be able to identify cues that suggest their children may be engaging in self-blame, practitioners could help parents understand which cues to look for in their children. Relevant skills would include understanding how to observe and note both behavioral and verbal red flags and developing the listening skills that would allow them to better identify any verbal messages that suggest self-blame or that the child believes they must prove their worth.

While everyone, regardless of their family structure, should work to develop healthy communication habits, for adolescent parents and their family members it is vital that they learn how to communicate with their children carefully, taking their specific family structure into consideration. For example, given the connection between one's perception of messages from their families and self-blame, a therapist or counselor could work with members of families of adolescent parents to help them learn how to communicate messages such as "having children at a young age is difficult" without also sending an underlying message of "I regret having you." Given the higher likelihood that those born to adolescent parents will become adolescent parents themselves, there could be value in communicating how difficult being an adolescent parent is, but those messages need to be tempered and communicated so that they do not lead to the child feeling guilty. Even though no one can ever guarantee children of adolescent parents will not interpret messages from their family in a negative way, certainly there are actions, such as encouraging parents to directly tell their children that they are not to blame, that adolescent parents can incorporate to try to decrease the likelihood children will interpret their messages about their families in a negative and self-focused manner.

Relatedly, given the importance of how those born to adolescent parents interpret the stories told to them, perhaps groups and organizations focused on supporting adolescent parents and their children could provide training to improve these family's storytelling techniques. Anything that would help people tell stories in a way that highlights the idea that parents made choices themselves and are therefore responsible for their own life outcomes, not their children, would be ideal. This type of training could increase the likelihood that parents have the skill to help ensure their children do not take on the blame for their parents' circumstances.

Advice for Researchers

For researchers interested in studying family stories, it is important to examine not just the storytelling process itself, but also what kind of circumstances engender the need for storytelling in the first place. Both the survey results and the interview findings from this study highlight the idea that experiences with stigmatization likely lead to the use of storytelling in families of adolescent parents and suggest that after both storytelling and stigmatization were accounted for in statistical models, only stigmatization remained a significant predictor of self-esteem. If stigma was not included in this study, the connections between stigma, storytelling, struggle, blame, and one's identity would not be clear. Therefore, without the inclusion of stigmatization in this study, the true influence of the stories themselves might not have been realized.

Previous research has consistently found a significant relationship between storytelling and both individual and family identity; however, the results of this study suggest this connection might be more nuanced for certain types of families, or at least for families with adolescent parents. For example, a storytelling-focused theory commonly utilized in family communication scholarship, Communicated Narrative Sensemaking theory (CNSM), focuses specifically on storytelling as a sensemaking tool and, therefore, only examines what happens as stories are being told, or after stories have been told. Thus, CNSM ignores what happens before stories are told, and what might lead to the use of storytelling in the first place (at least in the theoretical model). Results of the study highlighted in this book suggest that CNSM's focus on what happens post-storytelling might be too limited to truly understand *why* stories influence people the way they do in certain types of families.

Admittedly, scholars might say their goal is not to understand *why* stories influence but to explore *how* they do. The question then becomes, how much can researchers truly say about how stories influence people if they do not understand *why* stories would have an influence in the first place? There are a variety of experiences researchers could include as preceding events that might influence perceptions of stories. For example, in this study stigmatizing experiences, financial struggles, and parental relationship issues were all situations those born to adolescent parents reported witnessing that then influenced how they interpreted the stories they were told. Accounting for these three experiences in future scholarship would be a good place to start.

Additionally, it is important for scholars to consider how they themselves rate stories as either positive or negative. The results of this study suggest that sometimes the ratings of outside observers might not provide accurate representations of the perceptions individuals have of the stories they have been told. Therefore, future scholars who examine the influence of storytelling processes should consider asking participants themselves to rate the positivity or negativity of their family stories and utilize those self-ratings to see if personal perceptions of positivity or negativity predict family and life outcomes.

CONCLUDING THOUGHTS

The goal of this book is to better understand the roles that stigmatization of adolescent parenthood and the telling of birth/reproductive/origin stories have on those born to adolescent parents. The combination of survey responses and interview findings from children of adolescent parents helped to illuminate a clear picture of the ways stigmatization can harm not just the member of the family that has the stigmatizing characteristic, in this case, not only the adolescent parent but also other members of the family. Results also illustrate how children of adolescent parents are strongly affected by their perceptions of their parents and their families from a young age. Findings concerning participant awareness of their parents' stigmatized status and their own self-blame after seeing their parents' struggles illustrate how aware those born to adolescent parents are about their parents' circumstances.

Unfortunately, the interview findings also show that this awareness of their family's situation does not always lead to positive outcomes for children of adolescent parents. The awareness the interviewees described having, coupled with sensemaking skills typical of young children, meant that many children interpreted their family's struggles as being their fault. This self-blame led to guilt and became a filter through which they interpreted their world, including the stories they were told by family members. Thankfully, many of those born to adolescent parents, through family and/or outside support and an adjustment to how they understood their experiences, were able to redevelop their interpretations of their life experiences over time in a more positive manner. Specifically, as adults they were able to alter their understanding of their childhood experiences and work through their guilt, helping them understand that they are not responsible for their parents' choices, least of all their own existence, and they therefore have nothing to feel guilty about and nothing to prove.

As important as these insights are, the authors would be remiss in not reminding readers that while experiences described in this book show those born to adolescent parents may struggle due to circumstances related to their parents' age, the results should be interpreted carefully. The hope of the authors is that the ideas discussed here do not become just another negative talking point to support the claim that adolescent parenthood is problematic and/or that those born to adolescent parents are destined for difficult circumstances. Instead, the hope is that this book can be encouraging to family members of adolescent parents. To researchers, the authors hope this study encourages them to consider some ideas and connections between concepts that they might not have thought of previously. To practitioners, they hope the results have provided new ideas to consider with clients. To society in general, they hope that this study aids in helping people to be more aware of how they might unintentionally perpetuate stigma and cause harm. To adolescent parents and other family members, this research suggests how they can be an effective support system to those they likely care so much about. And lastly, to those born to adolescent parents themselves, the ideas here show they are not alone, and they are worthy. To them, the authors say, you are enough.

NOTE

1. A covariate is a variable that is not of direct interest to researchers but can influence the outcome of a statistical analysis (Keyton 2010).

References

Afifi, Tamara D., Davis, Shardé M., and Merril, Annie. 2014. "Single Parent Families: Creating a Sense of Family from Within." In *Remaking Family Communicatively*, edited by Leslie A. Baxter, 67–84. New York City: Peter Lang Publishing.

Barcelos, Christi A., and Gubrium, Aline C. 2014. "Reproducing Stories: Strategic Narratives of Teen Pregnancy and Motherhood." *Social Problems*, 61(3), 466–481. https://doi.org/10.1525/sp.2014.122an41.

Bartell Sheehan, Kim. 2018. "Crowdsourcing Research: Data Collection with Amazon's Mechanical Turk." *Communication Monographs*, 85(1), 140–156. https://doi.org/10.1080/03637751.2017.1342043.

Becker, Gay. 1997. *Disrupted Lives: How People Create Meaning in a Chaotic World*. Berkley: University of California Press.

Bisel, Ryan S., and Barge, J. Kevin. 2011. "Discursive Positioning and Planned Change in Organizations." *Human Relations*, 64(2), 257–283. https://doi.org/10.1177/0018726710375996.

Bisel, Ryan S., Barge, J. Kevin, Dougherty, Debbie S., Lucas, Kristen, and Tracy, Sarah J. 2014. "A Round-Table Discussion of 'Big' Data in Qualitative Organizational Communication Research." *Management Communication Quarterly*, 28(4), 625–649. https://doi.org/10.1177/0893318914549952.

Bostwick, Eryn N., & Johnson, Amy J. 2018. "A Measure for Discourse-Dependence: Quantitatively Examining Boundary Management Tactics Utilized by Discourse-Dependent Families." Paper presented at the *National Communication Association (NCA) Annual Conference: Communication at Play*, Salt Lake City, UT, November 8–11, 2018.

Brand, Gabrielle, Morrison, Paul, & Down, Barry. 2014. "How Do Health Professionals Support Pregnant and Young Mothers in the Community? A Selective Review of the Research Literature." *Women and Birth*, 27(3), 174–178. https://doi.org/10.1016/j.wombi.2014.05.004

Charmaz, Kathy. 2006. *Constructing Grounded Theory: A Practical Guide Through Qualitative Analysis*. Thousand Oaks: Sage.

Corrigan, Patrick W., and Miller, Frederick E. 2004. "Shame, Blame, and Contamination: A Review of the Impact of Mental Illness Stigma on Family Members." *Journal of Mental Health*, 13(6), 537–548. https://doi.org/10.1080/09638230400017004.

Creswell, John W. 2007. *Qualitative Inquiry and Research Design: Choosing Among Five Approaches*, 2nd ed. Thousand Oaks: Sage.

Edin, Kathryn, and Kefalas, Maria J. 2005. *Promises I Can Keep*. Berkley: University of California Press.

Fiese, Barbara H., and Winter, Marcia A. 2009. "Family Stories and Rituals." In *The Wiley-Blackwell Handbook of Family Psychology*, edited by James H. Bray, and Mark Stanton, 625–636. Malden: Wiley-Blackwell.

Fitzpatrick, Mary Anne, and Vangelisti, Anita L., eds. 1995. *Explaining Family Interactions*. Thousand Oaks: Sage.

Furstenberg, Frank. 2007. *Destinies of the Disadvantaged: The Politics of Teenage Childbearing*. New York: Sage.

Galvin, Kathleen. 2006. "Diversity's Impact on Defining the Family: Discourse-Dependence and Identity." In *The Family Communication Sourcebook*, edited by Lynn H. Turner, and Richard West, 3–19. Thousand Oaks: Sage.

Goffman, Erving. 1963. *Stigma: Notes on the Management of Spoiled Identity*. New York: Simon & Schuster.

Green, Sara E. 2003. "What Do You Mean 'What's Wrong with Her?': Stigma and the Lives of Families of Children with Disabilities." *Social Science & Medicine*, 57(8), 1361–1374. http://dx.doi.org/10.1016/S0277-9536(02)00511-7.

Haverfield, Marie C., and Theiss, Jennifer A. 2016. "Parents' Alcoholism Severity and Family Topic Avoidance about Alcohol as Predictors of Perceived Stigma Among Adult Children of Alcoholics: Implications for Emotional and Psychological Resilience." *Health Communication*, 31(6), 606–616. http://dx.doi.org/10.1080/10410236.2014.981665.

Hayden, Julia M., Singer, Jefferson A., and Chrisler, Joan C. 2006. "The Transmission of Birth Stories from Mother to Daughter: Self-Esteem and Mother-Daughter Attachment." *Sex Roles*, 55(5–6), 373–383. http://dx.doi.org/10.1007/s11199-006-9090-3.

Heider, Fritz. 1958. *The Psychology of Interpersonal Relations*. New York: Wiley.

Huisman, Dena. 2014. "Telling a Family Culture: Storytelling, Family Identity, and Cultural Membership." *Interpersona*, 8(2), 144–158. http://dx.doi.org/10.5964/ijpr.v8i2.152.

Huston, Ted L., McHale, Susan, M., and Crouter, Ann C. 1986. "When the Honeymoon's Over: Changes in the Marriage Relationship Over the First Year." In *The Emerging Field of Personal Relationships*, edited by Robin Gilmore and Steve Duck, 109–132. Hillsdale: Lawrence Erlbaum.

Joseph, Steven, and Linley, P. Alex. 2008. *Trauma, Recovery, and Growth: Positive Psychological Perspectives and Posttraumatic Stress*. Hoboken: John Wiley & Sons, Inc.

Kelly, Deirdre M. 1996. "Stigma Stories: Four Discourses about Teen Mothers, Welfare, and Poverty." *Youth and Society*, 27(4), 421–449. http://dx.doi.org/10.1177/0044118X96027004002.

Keyton, Joann. 2010. *Communication Research: Asking Questions, Finding Answers*, 3rd ed. New York: McGraw Hill.

Kiselica, Mark S. 2008. *When Boys Become Parents: Adolescent Fatherhood in America*. New Brunswick: Rutgers University Press.

Knapp, Mark L., Stohl, Cynthia, and Reardon, Kathleen K. 1981. "Memorable Messages." *Journal of Communication*, 31(4), 27–41. http://dx.doi.org/10.1111/j.1460-2466.1981.tb00448.x.

Koenig Kellas, Jody. 2005. "Family Ties: Communicating Identity Through Jointly Told Family Stories." *Communication Monographs*, 72(4), 365–389. https://doi.org/10.1080/03637750500322453.

Koenig Kellas, Jody, and Kranstuber Horstman, Haley. 2015. "Communicated Narrative Sensemaking: Understanding Family Narratives, Storytelling, and the Construction of Meaning Through a Communicative Lens." In *The SAGE Handbook of Family Communication*, edited by Lynn H. Turner, and Richard West, 76–90. Thousand Oaks: Sage.

Kornhaber, Rachel, Childs, Charmaine, and Cleary, Michelle. 2018. "Experiences of Guilt, Shame and Blame in those Affected by Burns: A Qualitative Systematic Review." *Burns*, 44(5), 1026–1039. http://dx.doi.org/10.1016/j.burns.2017.11.012.

Kouros, Chrystyna D., Wee, Sharyl E., Carson, Chelsea N., and Ekas, Naomi V. 2020. "Children's Self-Blame Appraisals About Their Mothers' Depressive Symptoms and Risk for Internalizing Symptoms." *Journal of Family Psychology*, 34(5), 534–543. http://dx.doi.org/10.1037/fam0000639.

Kranstuber, Haley, and Koenig Kellas, Jody. 2011. "'Instead of Growing Under Her Heart, I Grew in It': The Relationship Between Adoption Entrance Narratives and Adoptees' Self-Concept." *Communication Quarterly*, 59(2), 179–199. https://doi.org/10.1080/01463373.2011.563440.

Langellier, Kristin M., and Peterson, Eric E. 2006. "Family Storytelling as Communication Practice." In *The Family Communication Sourcebook*, edited by Lynn H. Turner, and Richard West, 109–128. Thousand Oaks: Sage.

Lindlof, Thomas R., and Taylor, Bryan C. 2011. *Qualitative Communication Research Methods*, 3rd ed. Thousand Oaks: Sage.

Manning, Wendy D., and Cohen, Jessica A. 2015. "Teenage Cohabitation, Marriage, and Childbearing." *Population Research and Policy Review*, 34(2), 161–177. http://dx.doi.org/10.1007/s11113-014-9341-x.

McAdams, Dan P. 1993. *The Stories We Live By: Personal Myths and the Making of the Self*. New York: Guilford Press.

McGraw, Kathleen M. 1987. "Guilt Following Transgression: An Attribution of Responsibility Approach." *Journal of Personality and Social Psychology*, 53(2), 247–256. http://dx.doi.org/10.1037/0022-3514.53.2.247.

Mead, George Herbert. 1934. *Mind, Self, and Society*. Chicago: University of Chicago Press.

Meisenbach, Rebecca J. 2010. "Stigma Management Communication: A Theory and Agenda for Applied Research on How Individuals Manage Moments of Stigmatized Identity." *Journal of Applied Communication Research*, 38(3), 268–292. https://doi.org/10.1080/00909882.2010.490841.

Mongeau, Paul A., Hale, Jerold L., and Alles, Marmy. 1994. "An Experimental Investigation of Accounts and Attributions Following Sexual Infidelity." *Communication Monographs*, 61(4), 326–344. https://doi.org/10.1080/03637759409376341.

Muhlbauer, Susan. 2002. "Experience of Stigma by Families with Mentally Ill Members." *Journal of the American Psychiatric Nurses Association*, 8(3), 76–83. https://doi.org/10.1067/mpn.2002.125222.

National Conference of State Legislatures. 2013. "Postcard: Teen Pregnancy Affects Graduation Rates." Accessed July 20, 2021. https://www.ncsl.org/research/health/teen-pregnancy-affects-graduation-rates-postcard.aspx.

Nordqvist, Petra. 2021. "Telling Reproductive Stories: Social Scripts, Relationality and Donor Conception." *Sociology*, 35(4), 677–695. https://doi.org/10.1177/0038038520981860.

Pescosolido, Bernice A., and Martin, Jack K. 2015. "The Stigma Complex." *Annual Review of Sociology*, 41(1), 87–116. https://doi.org/10.1146/annurev-soc-071312-145702.

Piaget, Jean. 1970. "Piaget's Theory." In *Carmichael's Manual of Child Psychology*, 3rd ed. Vol. 1, edited by Paul H. Mussen, 703–732. New York City: Wiley.

Rosenberg, Morris. 1979. *Conceiving the Self*. New York: Basic Books.

Rubin, Herbert J., and Rubin, Irene S. 2005. *Qualitative Interviewing: The Art of Hearing Data*, 2nd ed. Thousand Oaks: Sage.

Sedighimornani, Neda, Rimes, Katharine, and Verplanken, Bas. 2021. "Factors Contributing to the Experience of Shame and Shame Management: Adverse Childhood Experiences, Peer Acceptance, and Attachment Styles." *The Journal of Social Psychology*, 161(2), 1–17. https://doi.org/10.1080/00224545.2020.1778616.

Shaver, Kelly G. 1975. *An Introduction to Attribution Processes*. Cambridge: Winthrop Publishers.

SmithBattle, Lee I. 2013. "Reducing the Stigmatization of Teen Mothers." *The American Journal of Maternal Child Nursing*, 38(4), 235–241. http://dx.doi.org/10.1097/NMC.0b013e3182836bd4.

Stone, Elizabeth. 1988. *Black Sheep and Kissing Cousins: How our Family Stories Shape Us*. New York: Times Books.

Tangney, June Price. 1995. "Shame and Guilt in Interpersonal Relationships." In *Self-Conscious Emotions: The Psychology of Shame, Guilt, Embarrassment, and Pride*, edited by June Price Tangney, and Kurt W. Fischer, 114–139. New York City: Guilford Press.

Tolan, Patrick H., Gorman-Smith, Deborah, Huesmann, L. Rowell, and Zelli, Arnaldo. 1997. "Assessment of Family Relationship Characteristics: A Measure to Explain Risk for Antisocial Behavior and Depression Among Urban Youth." *Psychological Assessment*, 9(3), 212–223. https://doi.org/10.1037/1040-3590.9.3.212.

Wayne Leach, Colin. 2017. "Understanding Shame and Guilt." In *Handbook of the Psychology of Self-Forgiveness*, edited by Lydia Woodyatt, Everett L. Worthington, Jr., Michael Wenzel, and Brandon J. Griffin, 29–41. Cham: Springer.

Weisz, John R., and Stipek, Deborah J. 1982. "Competence, Contingency, and the Development of Perceived Control." *Human Development*, 25(4), 250–281. https://doi.org/10.1159/000272812.

Westman, Jack C. 2009. *Breaking the Adolescent Parent Cycle: Valuing Fatherhood and Motherhood*. Lanham: University Press of America.

Whitehead, Elizabeth. 2001. "Teenage Pregnancy: On the Road to Social Death." *International Journal of Nursing Studies*, 38(4), 437–446. https://doi.org/10.1016/S0020-7489(00)00086-9.

Whitley, Rob, and Kirmayer, Laurence J. 2008. "Perceived Stigmatisation of Young Mothers: An Exploratory Study of Psychological and Social Experience." *Social Science & Medicine*, 66(2), 339–348. http://dx.doi.org/10.1016/j.socscimed.2007.09.014.

Woodgate, Roberta L., Comaskey, Brenda, Tennent, Pauline, Wener, Pamela, and Altman, Gary. 2020. "The Wicked Problem of Stigma for Youth Living With Anxiety." *Qualitative Health Research*, 30(10), 1491–1502. https://doi.org/10.1177/1049732320916460.

Appendix A

Methodology

SURVEY METHODOLOGY

Data Collection

Data collection for the survey portion of the study took place in two phases. In the first phase, the authors utilized a variety of recruitment methods to reach individuals born to adolescent parents that met the inclusion criteria of the study to complete a survey. During the second phase, the first author interviewed a subset of survey participants in order to learn about their experiences growing up in more depth. This phase also provided context that allowed the authors to understand why the relationships they uncovered from the survey data were significant. Details about the inclusion criteria and recruitment methods to collect survey data are described next, followed by a description of the survey and the measures the authors used. Details about inclusion criteria and questions used for the interviews are described last.

To qualify to complete the survey, people needed to be between the ages of 18 and 64, born to at least one adolescent parent (aged 19 or younger at birth) and have grown up in a household with at least one biological parent or grandparent. These inclusion criteria were chosen for multiple reasons. First, an age range of 18–64 was chosen because the individuals born from 1954 to 2000 were either born or growing up during a time period when stigma against adolescent pregnancy was highest (Furstenberg 2007) and therefore would have been most likely to experience stigma and utilize family storytelling to mitigate that stigma. Research suggests that the adolescent pregnancy "epidemic" in US society (based on political policies and programs that have been established over time) began after the sexual revolution in the 1960s and seems to have peaked during the 1980s and 1990s (Furstenberg 2007). Based on research discussed earlier in this book that suggests the focus on adolescent pregnancy as an "epidemic" and "problem" has contributed to the stigmatization of adolescent parents, it is likely that those individuals alive between the 1960s and 1990s (i.e., during the time society was condemning adolescent pregnancy) experienced the most stigmatization/transfer of stigma.

Additionally, requiring that only one parent was an adolescent when the participant was born instead of both parents is important because a large percentage of children born to adolescent mothers have fathers who were over 19 when they were born (Kiselica 2008). If participation required that both parents were adolescents when the participant was born, those individuals born to an adolescent mother but older father would have been excluded even though their experiences are just as relevant to the purpose of the study. Finally, it was important to require participants to have grown up in a household with at least one biological parent or grandparent because the rationale of the research project was based on the influence of being born to an adolescent parent or adolescent parents on one's life. Individuals who did not spend time with their biological family members (e.g., were adopted) could face identity issues related to experiences other than having an adolescent parent or parents (Kranstuber and Koenig Kellas 2011). Therefore, this distinction was necessary to help ensure the outcomes the study examined were related to being born to adolescent parents, not other family structures or circumstances.

Participants for the study were recruited via a variety of IRB-approved methods. First, a recruitment description was posted on social media sites including Facebook, Twitter, and Reddit. The first author also sent a recruitment email out via a professional listserv for communication scholars and faculty (CRTNET), emailed 41 universities across the country asking for them to share the recruitment message with their students, emailed 52 organizations associated with adolescent pregnancy/parenthood describing the study and asking them to share the recruitment message with potential participants, and sent the recruitment message out to students directly at three different universities (one located in the South-Central United States, one in the Great Lakes region, and one in the southern United States). As compensation, those who completed the survey were placed in a drawing for one of ten $25.00 Amazon gift cards.

After six months of data collection, the methods described in the preceding text had not yet yielded a large enough number of participants to carry out the planned analyses (only 67 participant surveys came from these recruitment methods). To recruit more participants, the first author posted the study as a Human Intelligence Task (HIT) on MTurk. Workers on MTurk complete HITs in exchange for compensation, which, in this case, was US $2.00. Research suggests MTurk allows researchers to tap into a respondent pool that is diverse, and when researchers take precautions to ensure quality data, the data can be as valid and reliable as other data collection methods (Bartell Sheehan 2018).

For this study, three main precautions were taken. First, MTurk workers were only able to complete the HIT if they had a HIT approval rate of at least 95%, meaning throughout the time they had been working on MTurk, requesters had approved their work at least 95% of the time. Additionally, MTurkers only gained access to the survey after completing a short demographic screening survey, which served to make sure only those who qualified for the study were able to access it. Lastly, the first author included several attention check items in the survey, which required MTurkers to read carefully and answer questions in a particular way. Data from only those workers who answered the attention check items appropriately were retained for analysis.

Prior to choosing to participate, individuals were first able to read a description of the study, which described the study's purpose to better understand how storytelling processes in families influence family members. After reading the study description, potential participants were then able to access the survey via an online link (provided via Qualtrics) and were presented with an informed consent section that described the study in more detail. Those individuals who consented to participate were then taken to the survey questions. A copy of the survey questions can be found in Appendix C: Survey Questions. After completing the survey, individuals were provided with a link that displayed information about counseling services in their geographic region in case thinking about issues such as stigma and family stories caused them distress.

Three hundred and eight individuals opened the survey, but after data cleaning, only 141 were retained in the sample for future analyses. This difference in sample size occurred due to (1) individuals opening the survey without starting it ($n = 58$), (2) individuals completing the survey but not meeting the criteria for participation ($n = 70$), and (3) individuals starting the survey but not finishing at least 75% of it ($n = 39$). Importantly, out of the 141 individuals retained for data analysis, 67 were recruited using a method other than MTurk, while the remaining 74 were recruited using Mturk.[1] Demographic and descriptive details about these participants can be found in Appendix B: Descriptive Data About Research Participants.

Measures

The survey contained a mix of open- and closed-ended questions that enabled the authors to examine the relationships between experiences with stigma, birth/reproductive/origin stories people remember hearing, and self-esteem. As part of the survey, participants indicated whether they would be willing to participate in a follow-up interview to provide more information about the answers they provided in the survey. Those that completed the survey via MTurk were not asked this question due to restrictions placed on requesters by Amazon (i.e., no contact with workers outside the MTurk platform is allowed). Details about the measures used for the survey portion of the data collection process can be found next, while information about participants, procedures, and measures for the interview portion of the study can be found later.

Family satisfaction was measured using a modified version of Huston, McHale, and Crouter's (1986) Marital Opinion Questionnaire. The scale was modified so that participants were asked to identify their feelings toward their family members instead of their marital partner. The measure contains 11 items, 10 on a 7-point semantic differential scale (e.g., miserable—enjoyable, rewarding—disappointing) and one 7-point Likert scale item assessing relational satisfaction more globally (1 = completely satisfied, 7 = completely dissatisfied).

Family closeness was measured using Tolan et al.'s (1997) family relations scale, which contains six items on a 1–5 Likert scale (1 = not true, 5 = always true). Example items include, "I was available when others in the family want to talk to me" and "Family members felt very close to each other."

Family cohesion was measured using Tolan et al.'s (1997) cohesion scale, which consists of nine items on a 1–5 Likert scale (1 = definitely false, 5 = definitely true). Example items include, "There was little group spirit in our family" (reverse coded) and "Family members really backed each other up."

Self-esteem was measured utilizing Rosenberg's (1979) Self-Esteem Scale (RSES). The RSES is a 10-item measure on a 4-point Likert scale (1 = strongly disagree, 4 = strongly agree), with higher scores indicating higher levels of self-esteem. Sample items include, "I feel I have a number of good qualities" and "On the whole, I am satisfied with myself."

Questions concerning participants' experiences with stigma covered two stigma-related experiences: their parents' experiences of being stigmatized and their personal experiences with stigmatization. Additionally, because previous research suggests family members of those who are stigmatized may fear that their family member's stigma will influence how others see them (Goffman 1963), participants were also asked how concerned they were about their parents' experience with stigma influencing how others viewed them. All the questions related to stigma were developed by the first author.

Before being presented with questions about each of the two stigma-related experiences described previously, participants were presented with a definition of stigmatization. This section defined stigmatization as "being judged or treated differently." Then, participants were asked whether they remembered their parent(s) being judged differently because of how old they were when they had children (Yes or No). If they chose "Yes," they were asked to rate how damaging that experience was for their parents on a scale of 0–100.

Next, respondents were asked to answer questions concerning their parents' experiences with stigmatization. They were asked to describe an example of a time their parent(s) were treated differently because of how old they were when they had children, then they were asked to indicate how often their parent(s) were concerned about being treated differently. How often their parent(s) were concerned with being treated differently was measured using five questions on a 1–5 Likert scale (1 = never, 5 = always). Example questions are, "How often do you remember your parent(s) feeling worried about people treating them differently because of their age when they had children?" and "How often do you remember your parent(s) feeling anxious about people treating them differently because of their age when they had children?"

Then, participants were asked questions related to whether they were concerned that the stigma their parent(s) experienced would influence how others viewed them, personally. The questions were measured utilizing the same statements used to measure how often their parents were concerned with their own treatment (described earlier), except slightly reworded to reflect this new context. For example, "How often do you remember your parent(s) feeling worried about people treating them differently because of their age when they had children?" was changed to, "How often do you remember feeling worried that your parents' age would influence how people viewed you?" As before, these five questions were measured on a 1–5 Likert scale (1 = never, 5 = always).

Lastly, participants were asked whether they remembered being stigmatized because of their parents' age when they were born (Yes or No). If they indicated being stigmatized, they were asked to rate how damaging that stigmatization was to them on a scale of 0–100 and asked to provide an example of a time they were stigmatized because of their parents' age when they were born. The last part of the stigmatization section used the same five questions described in the previous two sections, reworded to reflect their own stigma and not the stigma their parent(s) experienced. For example, the question, "How often do you remember your parent(s) feeling anxious about people treating them differently because of their age when they had children?" was changed to, "How often do you remember feeling anxious about people treating you differently because of your parents' age when you were born?" As before, these five questions were measured on a 1–5 Likert scale (1 = never, 5 = always).

Discourse-dependent boundary management techniques were measured using items created by the first author. Participants were first presented with a statement that explained they would be presented with five different behaviors they and their family members may or may not have engaged in while they were growing up, and that they would be provided with a definition of each behavior. Participants were also told they would be given a hypothetical scenario that depicted each behavior and would be asked to indicate how often they and their family members engaged in each behavior. After careful consideration, the authors chose to include questions that represented all external boundary management tactics,[2] but only storytelling as an internal boundary management tactic. This choice was made for three main reasons. First, the authors considered how each tactic might be carried out in families of adolescent parents. Second, based on that understanding, they considered whether individuals from these families would be likely to engage in each tactic. Third, given the focus of storytelling in this study and not on the other internal processes families may engage in, examining only narrating seemed appropriate for the scope of the research.

After being presented with a definition and scenario associated with each of the boundary management tactics mentioned previously, participants were asked to rate how frequently they or their family members engaged in similar interactions throughout their lives. Frequency was measured using four items on a 5-point semantic differential scale developed by the first author. Opposing points were "infrequently" versus "frequently," "often" versus "not often," "rarely" versus "regularly," and "always" versus "never." Because no one has measured boundary management tactics before, prior to her recent passing the authors shared these items with Kathleen Galvin, the scholar credited with the development of the concept of discourse-dependent families. The goal was to get feedback from Dr. Galvin regarding the face validity of the items. Feedback from Galvin suggested the items did, indeed, have face validity.

Questions concerning experiences with storytelling were asked utilizing a combination of open- and closed-ended questions. First, participants were asked whether they remembered being told a story, or stories, about their conception, their mother's pregnancy, and/or their birth (Yes or No). Those who answered "Yes" were then asked (1) to describe how they came to hear the stories, (2) to describe one of the stories in detail, and (3) to rate the story's positivity. Story positivity was assessed using four items on a 5-point semantic differential scale developed by the author. Opposing points were "very positive" versus "very negative," "unhappy" versus "happy," "pleased" versus "displeased," and "dissatisfied" versus "satisfied."

Lastly, participants were provided with an open-ended question asking them to describe the most influential story they were told by their family (again, a story centered on their birth, their mother's pregnancy, or their conception) and were asked to rate the positivity of the story utilizing the same semantic differential scale described to measure story positivity above.

Table A.1 provides information regarding the means, standard deviations, and alpha reliabilities for all scales used in the survey. Importantly, prior to engaging in any analyses, the first author conducted a confirmatory factor analysis (CFA) to examine how the items used in the survey related to one another and related to the latent variables they were intended to measure. This also allowed the authors to drop any items that might not be measuring the intended latent factors from future analyses, thereby increasing the validity of the results. Details associated with this CFA are not reported here but can be provided to the reader by emailing the first author at the following email address: e.bostwick@tcu.edu. Table A.2 provides details to show how the reliability of the scales changed after completing the CFA.

Survey Analysis

Although the study's focus was the influence of stigmatization due to being born to an adolescent parent(s), there are other factors that could influence why someone is stigmatized, and these factors may correlate with being an adolescent parent. For example, socioeconomic status and race/ethnicity could play a role in why someone is stigmatized, and research has found connections between these demographic characteristics and rates of adolescent pregnancy (Furstenberg 2007). Therefore, when analyzing the survey data, when possible the authors chose to control for a variety of demographic

Table A.1 Means, Standard Deviations, and Reliabilities for all Survey Scales

Latent Variable	Range	M	SD	α
Family Satisfaction	1–7	4.55	1.59	0.95
Family Closeness	1–5	3.29	1.18	0.83
Family Cohesion	1–5	3.33	1.20	0.88
Self-Esteem	1–4	2.91	0.72	0.93
Parental Concern for Own Stigma	1–5	1.93	0.96	0.96
Participant Concern for Parental Stigma	1–5	2.02	1.07	0.95
Participant Concern for Own Stigma	1–5	1.87	1.02	0.96
Labeling	1–5	2.36	1.34	0.96
Explaining	1–5	3.02	1.36	0.95
Legitimizing	1–5	2.56	1.35	0.95
Defending	1–5	2.35	1.26	0.95
Narrating	1–5	2.97	1.28	0.94
Positivity Story 1	1–5	3.03	1.09	0.95
Positivity Story 2	1–5	3.28	1.23	0.96

Notes. Positivity Story 1 refers to participants' assessment of the positivity of a story they indicated hearing while growing up, while Positivity Story 2 refers to participants' assessment of the positivity of the most influential story they heard growing up. Higher scores on each of the scales mean the participant has indicated more of the variable being measured, that is, more family satisfaction, more engagement in labeling, and so on.

Table A.2   Reliabilities for Scales Before and After the CFA

Latent Variable	Alpha Reliability Pre-CFA	Alpha Reliability Post-CFA
Family Satisfaction	0.95	0.96
Family Closeness	0.83	0.93
Family Cohesion	0.88	0.90
Self-Esteem	0.93	0.92
Parental Concern for Own Stigma	0.96	0.96
Participant Concern for Parental Stigma	0.95	0.95
Participant Concern for Own Stigma	0.96	0.96
Labeling	0.96	0.96
Explaining	0.95	0.95
Legitimizing	0.95	0.95
Defending	0.95	0.95
Narrating	0.94	0.94
Positivity Story 1	0.95	0.95
Positivity Story 2	0.96	0.96

Notes. Positivity Story 1 refers to participants' assessment of the positivity of a story they indicated hearing while growing up, while Positivity Story 2 refers to participants' assessment of the positivity of the most influential story they heard growing up.

characteristics associated with race/ethnicity and socioeconomic status (ethnicity, level of education for the participant, level of education for the participant's parents [when the participant was born, while they were growing up, and currently], and the parental figures in the household in which the participant grew up) in the analyses.

Additionally, particularly when examining outcomes such as self-esteem and family satisfaction, other concepts such as family closeness and family cohesion could also have an influence on the relationships tested. Therefore, to eliminate the influence of family closeness and family cohesion, as well as in order to make sure all analyses utilized the same control variables, when possible the authors also controlled for these two concepts. Furthermore, because one's personal experience with stigma is likely influenced by their parents' experiences with stigma (and vice versa), any analysis that examined outcomes associated with one of these stigmatization processes controlled for the influence of the other. For example, an analysis that examined the effect of one's parent being stigmatized controlled for the effect of being stigmatized personally.

Although this book does not present information in the form of hypotheses and research questions, to be transparent a list of all research questions and hypotheses associated with the quantitative portion of data collection is provided next, along with a brief description of how each was analyzed. More information regarding analytical decisions can be provided to the reader by contacting the first author at the following email address: e.bostwick@tcu.edu. Hypotheses and research questions were:

H1: Individuals born to adolescent parents are more likely to view their parents as stigmatized than view themselves as stigmatized. Tested using a chi-square test of independence.

H2: The more often individuals remember their parents worrying about the stigma of being an adolescent parent, the more often they will report (1) feeling worried about their parents' stigmatization influencing how others viewed them and (2) feeling worried about being stigmatized themselves. Tested using two hierarchical regressions.

H3: Individuals who report being stigmatized because their parent(s) were adolescents when they were born will have lower self-esteem than those that do not report being stigmatized. Tested using an ANCOVA.

H4: Individuals who report that their parent(s) were stigmatized because they were adolescents when they were born will have lower self-esteem than those who do not report their parents were stigmatized. Tested using an ANCOVA.

H5: The more frequently participants remember (1) feeling worried about their parents' stigmatization influencing how others viewed them, and (2) feeling worried about being stigmatized themselves, the lower their self-esteem will be. Tested using a hierarchical regression.

RQ1: Do individuals born to adolescent parents report engaging in certain boundary management tactics more frequently than others? Answered by calculating mean scores for each boundary management tactic, developing 95% confidence intervals around each mean score, and comparing those confidence intervals to one another to see whether they overlapped.

H6: Those who report that their parents were stigmatized because of their family form are more likely to engage in boundary management tactics ([1] labeling, [2] explaining, [3] legitimizing, [4] defending, and [5] narrating) than those who report their parents were not stigmatized. Tested using a MANCOVA.

RQ2: What proportion of children of adolescent parents report hearing their birth/origin stories from their family throughout their lives? Answered by examining descriptive statistics.

H7: Individuals' ratings of the positivity of their birth/origin story will be related to their self-esteem and family satisfaction such that the more positive an individual rates their story (1) the higher their self-esteem and (2) the higher their family satisfaction. Tested using two hierarchical regressions.

H8: Valence of one's birth/origin story will moderate the relationship between stigmatization and self-esteem such that those individuals who report that their parents were stigmatized for being an adolescent parent and who rate their birth/origin story more positively will have higher self-esteem than those who report that their parents were stigmatized for being an adolescent parent and who rate their birth/origin story more negatively. Tested using the Hayes PROCESS macro simple moderation analysis.

H9: Valence of birth/origin story will moderate the relationship between stigmatization and self-esteem such that those individuals who report they were stigmatized due to the age of their parent(s) when they were born and who rate their birth/origin story more positively will have higher self-esteem than those who report they were stigmatized due to the age of their parent(s) when they were born and who rate their birth/origin story more negatively. Tested using the Hayes PROCESS macro simple moderation analysis.

INTERVIEW METHODOLOGY

Data Collection

Participants for the interview portion of data collection were individuals who (1) indicated in their survey responses that they would be willing to participate in a follow-up interview, (2) provided contact information for a follow-up, (3) reported that either they or their parents were stigmatized growing up due to their parent(s) age when they were born, and (4) reported hearing a birth, reproductive, or origin story that they indicated clearly was positive or negative (based on self-reported ratings) in tone and which they also indicated was influential in their life. These criteria were chosen because it was important that anyone who participated in interviews was able to speak about the influence of their experiences with stigma and storytelling on their lives. As previously mentioned, the goal of this analysis was to provide context so that the authors could understand *why* experiences with stigma and storytelling influenced participants' identities the way that they did. Therefore, only those participants who reported experiences with both stigma and storytelling were relevant for this portion of data collection.

Additionally, participants with stories that they rated as having a clear positive or negative tone were necessary given the importance of the tone of the story to the outcomes examined in the study and the basics of Communicated Narrative Sensemaking theory. The goal was to understand how positively and negatively rated stories influence identity, so interviewing participants who experienced clearly positive or clearly negative stories and described them as influential was important. These criteria described here also helped to ensure the collection of interview data was guided by theoretical sampling, which is an important part of the interview process (Lindlof and Taylor 2011).

Out of the 141 participants who qualified for and completed the survey, 27 indicated they would be willing to be contacted for a follow-up interview. Fifteen of these participants met the criteria to be selected for an interview. All 15 of these individuals were sent an IRB-approved email providing information about the follow-up interview and asking potential participants to contact the researcher if they were interested in moving forward to schedule an interview, or if they had any concerns or questions. The email also let them know they would receive a $20 Amazon gift card if they completed an interview as compensation for their time. Of the 15 people who were contacted, 8 individuals responded and agreed to participate in the follow-up interview. Demographic and descriptive details about those who participated in the interview can be found in Appendix B: Descriptive Data About Research Participants.

Interview Script

After consenting to participate and refusing the option to opt out of the study, all eight individuals partook in interviews with the first author asking them questions related to their experiences as a child of adolescent parents (or in some cases one adolescent parent), their experiences with stigma due to their parent(s)' age when they were born, the influence their birth/reproductive/origin story had on their identity growing up, and how their understanding of their birth/reproductive/origin story had changed over time. The interviews were semi-structured to allow participants to answer in a variety of different ways and to make sure the first author did not ask questions that were so specific to the research questions that the participants felt like they needed to answer in any certain way. Also, Rubin and Rubin (2005) have suggested that the use of open-ended questions gives participants the opportunity to provide a thick description of their experiences, which is essential when conducting qualitative research. If the participants did not provide sufficient information when answering the general questions, probes were used to encourage more disclosure. The interviews took place over the phone and were also audio-recorded and transcribed. All participants are identified by a pseudonym instead of their real name, and all identifying information has been kept confidential. After participating in interviews lasting about 30–40 minutes, the participants were thanked for their participation and emailed their $20 Amazon gift card. See Appendix D: Interview Schedule for a list of the exact questions used in the interview. Research questions associated with the interview portion of data collection were:

RQ3: How do those born to adolescent parents describe their childhood?

RQ4: While growing up, how do those born to adolescent parents describe the influence of their birth/origin story (or stories) on their identity?

RQ5: How do those born to adolescent parents describe the way their understanding of their birth/origin story (or stories) has changed over time?

Data Analysis

The interviews produced about 111 single-spaced pages of transcription for analysis. To identify themes, a modified version of constant comparative analysis was used. This analysis aims to develop themes and trends based on answers participants give (Charmaz 2006). Usually, the analysis ends with the proposition of a theory or model developed from the data (Lindlof and Taylor 2011). To carry out this analysis, the first author separated those portions of data that did not pertain to the research questions from those portions of data that were relevant. Portions of data that were deemed irrelevant to the research questions were deleted from the transcript pages, while relevant data were retained. This process is known as data reduction (Bisel et al. 2014) and helps ensure the researcher only analyses data that is applicable to the research questions. The data reduction process resulted in a total of 58 single-spaced pages of transcription.

Next, the first author began open coding (Lindlof and Taylor 2011) by reading through the relevant utterances with the goal of understanding what each participant was trying to convey. As the codes were created, the first author also made memos, which allowed them to record any thoughts that came to mind during the process, as well as write down any similarities between the codes. Open coding ended when all responses had a code. The codes developed through open coding were then compared to one another so that the first author could combine similar codes into broader categories (Lindlof and Taylor 2011). After making several passes through the data during this phase, the first author then reduced the categories so that they were more parsimonious. Categories were reduced by examining each original category, comparing each category to the others, and combining those that were similar in nature.

The last phase the first author went through was axial coding, in which the goal was to figure out how categories were connected and what the big picture was (i.e., what were the data saying about this phenomenon; Lindlof and Taylor 2011). Axial coding ended when no new connections between the categories were made. Lastly, the first author also engaged in two credibility checks in order to ensure the integrity of the analysis. First, a negative case analysis was utilized (Bisel and Barge 2011), which occurs when researchers use a disconfirming case to refine a hypothesis. In these cases, when certain responses do not fit into the categories researchers have developed, they might actually be used to support the hypothesis they have developed instead of refuting it. Second, the first author engaged in member checking with two of the interview participants, which occurs when researchers ask the participants to comment about the perceived credibility of the findings and interpretations (Creswell 2007). Questions about any methodological or analytical choices made by the researchers should be directed to the first author at the following email address: e.bostwick@tcu.edu.

NOTES

1. The first author utilized an item in the survey that distinguished which source participants used to access their survey (i.e., Facebook, Twitter, Reddit, organizations, university LISTSERVs, CRTNET, or MTurk) to statistically examine whether there were significant demographic differences between groups based on source, as well as to check whether source of one's survey influenced any of the variables used to test hypotheses and research questions. Results revealed no significant differences based on source of participants; therefore, source was not used as a control variable.

2. Galvin (2006) developed four external boundary management tactics that she said people used to communicate about their family form with outsiders, and four internal boundary management tactics that she said people used to communicate about their family form with other family members. Storytelling is the only boundary management tactic described in detail in this book but given that the scope of the research project was larger, the authors created measures for the external boundary management tactics as well. Information about those tactics can be found in Galvin (2006). See Bostwick and Johnson (2018) to learn more about the scale referenced here.

Appendix B

Descriptive Data About Research Participants

SURVEY PARTICIPANTS

Participants ranged in age from 18 to 64 ($M = 30.11$, $SD = 10.53$). The sample was 67.38% female ($n = 95$), with 31.91% males ($n = 45$), and one participant who preferred not to answer the question. Over 90% of participants had a mother who was 19 or younger when they were born (90.78%, $n = 128$), while 49.6% of participants had a father who was 19 or younger when they were born ($n = 70$).

About 44% of participants' biological parents were married when they were born (43.97%, $n = 62$), 34.75% were in a relationship ($n = 49$), 8.51% were separated ($n = 12$), 5.67% were cohabiting ($n = 8$), and 7.09% either did not know their parents' relationship when they were born or listed another type of relationship ($n = 10$).

Close to 42% of participants indicated that their biological parents were married while they were growing up (41.84%, $n = 59$), 24.82% said they were never married ($n = 35$), 14.89% said they were divorced while they were growing up ($n = 21$), 9.93% said they were divorced and remarried ($n = 14$), 5.67% said they were cohabiting ($n = 8$), and 2.84% indicated some other parental relationship ($n = 4$).

About 26% indicated that their parents were currently married (26.24%, $n = 37$), 21.28% said they were never married ($n = 30$), 16.31% said they were currently divorced ($n = 23$), 14.18% said they were divorced and remarried ($n = 20$), 8.51% were widowed ($n = 12$), 2.84% were cohabiting ($n = 4$), and 10.64% were in another type of relationship ($n = 15$).

About half of the participants grew up in a household with their biological parents (49.65%, $n = 70$), 23.40% grew up in a household with one biological parent and a stepparent ($n = 33$), 19.86% grew up in a household with a single parent ($n = 28$), and 7.09% said they grew up in some other household structure ($n = 10$). The average household size (number of family members within the household) was 4.66, $SD = 1.77$.

Most of the participants identified as Caucasian (64.54%, $n = 91$), 12.77% identified as African American ($n = 18$), 9.9% identified as Hispanic or Latino ($n = 14$), 7.80% identified as Asian ($n = 11$), one participant identified as Native American, and 4.26% listed "Other" as their racial/ethnic identity ($n = 6$). Almost 40% of participants completed some college (39.01%, $n = 55$), 21.99% earned a four-year college degree ($n = 31$), 12.77% earned a master's degree ($n = 18$), 12.06% earned a two-year college degree ($n = 17$), 9.93% earned a high school degree or GED ($n = 14$), 2.13% did not earn a high school degree ($n = 3$), and 2.13% earned a doctoral degree ($n = 3$).

The majority of participants mothers' (51.77%, $n = 73$) and fathers' (50.35%, $n = 71$) highest level of education when they were born was a high school diploma or GED, followed by less than high school (36.87%$_{mother}$, $n = 52$; 31.21%$_{father}$, $n = 44$), some college (8.51%$_{mother}$, $n = 12$; 10.64%$_{father}$, $n = 15$), and a two-year degree (1.42%$_{mother}$, $n = 2$; 1.42%$_{father}$, $n = 2$). No one's mother had a four-year degree at their birth; however, 4.96% of participants indicated their father did ($n = 7$). No one indicated that either of their parents had a master's, doctoral, or professional degree at their birth and two people left educational information for their fathers at their birth blank.

Education information for participants' parents was also measured while they were growing up. Most participants mothers' (43.26%, $n = 61$) and fathers' (48.23%, $n = 68$) highest level of education while they were growing up was a high school diploma or GED. For mothers, the next most common level of education while the participant was growing up was some college (21.28%, $n = 30$), followed by less than high school (17.73%, $n = 25$), a two-year degree (9.22% $n = 13$), a four-year degree (5.67%, $n = 8$), and a master's degree (2.84%, $n = 4$). No one's mother had a doctoral degree or professional degree while they were growing up. For fathers, the next most common level of education while the participant was growing up was less than high school (21.99%, $n = 31$), followed by some college (12.06% $n = 17$), a four-year degree (9.93%, $n = 14$), a two-year degree (4.26%, $n = 6$), a master's degree (1.42%, $n = 2$), and one participant indicated their father had a doctoral degree. No one's father had a professional degree while they were growing up. Two individuals left this information about their father's education blank.

Lastly, each participant also indicated their parents' highest level of education at the time the data were collected. At this point, most participants still identified a high school diploma or GED as the highest level of education for their mother (41.13%, $n = 58$) and father (46.81%, $n = 66$). For mothers, the next most common level of education when the data were collected was some college (19.86%, $n = 28$), followed by a two-year degree (12.06%, $n = 17$), less than high school (11.35% $n = 16$), a four-year degree (10.64%, $n = 15$), and a master's degree (4.96%, $n = 7$). No one's mother had a doctoral degree or professional degree at the time of data collection. For fathers, the next most common level of education at the time of data collection was less than high school (17.73%, $n = 25$), followed by some college (12.77% $n = 18$), a four-year degree (12.06%, $n = 17$), a two-year degree (4.96%, $n = 7$), a master's degree (2.13%, $n = 3$), and one participant indicated their father had a doctoral degree. No one's father had a professional degree at the time of data collection. Again, two individuals left this information about their father's education blank.

INTERVIEW PARTICIPANTS

A total of eight people participated in the interviews. Based on the data provided in their surveys, seven interviewees were female and one was male. They ranged in age from 19 to 57 ($M = 33$, $SD = 13.58$) and 62.50% were Caucasian ($n = 5$), 25.00% were African American ($n = 2$), and 12.50% identified as Hispanic or Latino ($n = 1$). Half of the interview participants said their parents were married when they were born (50.00%, $n = 4$), 37.50% said their parents were in a relationship ($n = 3$), and 12.50% said they were cohabiting ($n = 1$). While they were growing up, 62.50% said their parents were married ($n = 5$), 25.00% said they were never married ($n = 2$), and 12.50% listed their parents' relationship while growing up as "Other" ($n = 1$). Half of interviewees said their parents are currently married (50.00%, $n = 4$), 25.00% said they were never married ($n = 2$), 12.50% said they are divorced ($n = 1$), and 12.50% listed their parents' current relationship as "Other" ($n = 1$). While growing up, 62.50% of people said they were in a household with both biological parents ($n = 5$), 25.00% said they grew up in a single-parent household ($n = 2$), and 12.50% described the parental figures in their household as "Other" ($n = 1$), elaborating that they grew up with their mother and maternal grandparents. About 37.50% of interviewees had a four-year college degree ($n = 3$), 37.50% had a master's degree ($n = 3$), 12.50% said they attended some college ($n = 1$), and 12.50% had a doctoral degree ($n = 1$).

Most interviewees mothers' (50%, $n = 4$) and fathers' (62.5%, $n = 5$) highest level of education when they were born was a high school diploma or GED, followed by less than high school (37.5%$_{mother}$, $n = 3$; 25%$_{father}$, $n = 2$) and some college (12.5%$_{mother}$, $n = 1$; 12.5%$_{father}$, $n = 1$). No one indicated that either of their parents had a two-year, four-year, master's, doctoral, or professional degree at their birth.

Most participants mothers' (37.5%, $n = 3$) and fathers' (50%, $n = 4$) highest level of education while they were growing up was a high school diploma or GED. For mothers, the next most common level of education while the participant was growing up was some college (25%, $n = 2$), followed by less than high school (12.5%, $n = 1$), a two-year degree (12.5% $n = 1$), and a four-year degree (12.5% $n = 1$). No interviewees' mother had a master's degree, a doctoral degree, or a professional degree while they were growing up. For fathers, the next most common level of education while the participant was growing up was a four-year degree (25%, $n = 2$), followed by less than high school (12.5%, $n = 1$), and a doctoral degree (12.5%, $n = 1$).

At the point the data were collected, most interviewees still identified a high school diploma or GED as the highest level of education for their mother (50%, $n = 4$) and father (37.5%, $n = 3$). For mothers, the next most common level of education when the data were collected was a two-year degree (25%, $n = 2$), followed by some college (12.5%, $n = 1$), and a four-year degree (12.5%, $n = 1$). No one's mother had less than a high school education, a master's degree, a doctoral degree, or a professional degree at the time of data collection. For fathers, the next most common level of education at the time of data collection was a four-year degree (25%, $n = 2$), followed by less than high school (12.5%, $n = 1$), a master's degree ($n = 1$), and a doctoral degree (12.5%, $n = 1$). No one's father had some college, a two-year degree, or a professional degree at the time of data collection. No one's father had some college, a two-year degree, or a master's degree at the time of data collection.

Appendix C

Survey Questions

This appendix is a list of all of the items included in the survey. Items are presented in the same order and with the same descriptions that survey participants saw when they completed the survey itself.

Please answer the following demographic questions.
What is your biological sex? Male Female
How old are you in years (e.g., 28)?_____
How old, in years (e.g., 19), was **your mother** when you were born?_____
How old, in years (e.g., 19), was **your father** when you were born?_____
What race/ethnicity best describes you?

African American
Caucasian
Hispanic or Latino
Asian
Native Hawaiian or Other Pacific Islander
Native American
Other _____

Which description below best describes the relationship between your biological parents **when you were born**?

Married
In a relationship
Cohabiting
Separated
Unknown
Other _____

Which description below best describes the relationship between your biological parents **while you were growing up?**

Married
In a relationship
Cohabiting
Separated
Unknown
Other _____

Which description best describes the relationship between your biological parents **currently?**

Married
In a relationship
Cohabiting
Separated
Unknown
Other _____

What is the highest level of education you have completed?

Less than High School
High School/GED
Some College
two-year College Degree
four-year College Degree
Master's Degree
Doctoral Degree
Professional Degree

What is the highest level of education **your mother had completed when you were born?**

Less than High School
High School / GED
Some College
Two-year College Degree
Four-year College Degree
Master's Degree
Doctoral Degree
Professional Degree

What is the highest level of education **your mother had completed when you were growing up?**

Less than High School
High School/GED
Some College
Two-year College Degree
Four-year College Degree
Master's Degree
Doctoral Degree
Professional Degree

What is the highest level of education **your mother has completed as of now?**

Less than High School
High School/GED
Some College
Two-year College Degree
Four-year College Degree
Master's Degree
Doctoral Degree
Professional Degree

What is the highest level of education **your father had completed when you were born?**

Less than High School
High School/GED
Some College
Two-year College Degree
Four-year College Degree
Master's Degree
Doctoral Degree
Professional Degree

What is the highest level of education your father had completed when you were **growing up?**

Less than High School
High School/GED
Some College

Two-year College Degree
Four-year College Degree
Master's Degree
Doctoral Degree
Professional Degree

What is the highest level of education **your father has completed as of now**?

Less than High School
High School/GED
Some College
Two-year College Degree
Four-year College Degree
Masters Degree
Doctoral Degree
Professional Degree

In which state do you currently reside?
In which state did you grow up?
Please choose the option that best describes the parental figures in the household you grew up in.

Biological Parents
Biological Parent and a Stepparent
Adoptive Parents
Single Parent
Other _____

Please indicate the number of people in the household in which you grew up. Please use numerals (i.e., 7).

For all of the questions in this section please think about your relationship with your family members from the house in which you grew up. Please choose the options that most closely describes your feelings toward those family members.

Miserable -- -- -- -- -- -- -- Enjoyable
Hopeful -- -- -- -- -- -- -- Discouraging
Free -- -- -- -- -- -- -- Tied Down
Empty -- -- -- -- -- -- -- Full
Interesting -- -- -- -- -- -- -- Boring
Rewarding -- -- -- -- -- -- -- Disappointing
Doesn't give me much chance -- -- -- -- -- -- -- Brings out the best in me

Lonely -- -- -- -- -- -- -- Friendly
Hard -- -- -- -- -- -- -- Easy
Worthwhile -- -- -- -- -- -- -- Useless

All things considered, how satisfied have you been with your relationship with your family members from the house in which you grew up?

Completely Dissatisfied   2   3   Neutral   5   6   Completely Satisfied

Please answer the following questions regarding the level of closeness between those who resided in the household you grew up in. **While answering these questions please do so based on your experiences growing up, NOT your experiences currently.**

Family members really helped and supported one another.

Definitely False   2   Neither True Nor False   4   Definitely True

We often seemed to be killing time at home.

Definitely False   2   Neither True Nor False   4   Definitely True

We put a lot of energy into what we did at home.

Definitely False   2   Neither True Nor False   4   Definitely True

There was a feeling of togetherness in our family.

Definitely False   2   Neither True Nor False   4   Definitely True

We rarely volunteered when something had to be done at home.

Definitely False   2   Neither True Nor False   4   Definitely True

Family members really backed each other up.

Definitely False   2   Neither True Nor False   4   Definitely True

There was little group spirit in our family.

Definitely False   2   Neither True Nor False   4   Definitely True

We really got along well with each other.

Definitely False   2   Neither True Nor False   4   Definitely True

There was plenty of time and attention for everyone in our family.

Definitely False   2   Neither True Nor False   4   Definitely True

Please click on the picture that best describes the relationship you have with those who lived in the household you grew up in. Please answer this question based on your experiences growing up, NOT your experiences currently.

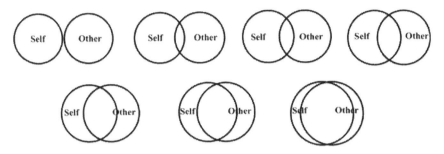

Please answer the following questions about those that lived in the household you grew up in. While answering these questions please do so based on your experiences growing up, NOT your experiences currently.

We could easily think of things to do together as a family.

  Not True   2   Neutral   4   Always True

Family members felt very close to each other.

  Not True   2   Neutral   4   Always True

Family members asked each other for help.

  Not True   2   Neutral   4   Always True

I was available when others in the family wanted to talk to me.

  Not True   2   Neutral   4   Always True

Family members liked to spend free time with each other.

  Not True   2   Neutral   4   Always True

I listened to what other family members had to say even when I disagreed.

  Not True   2   Neutral   4   Always True

Below is a list of statements dealing with your general feelings about yourself. Please indicate how strongly you agree or disagree with each statement.

On the whole, I am satisfied with myself.

  Strongly Disagree   Disagree   Agree   Strongly Agree

At times I think I am no good at all.

    Strongly Disagree   Disagree   Agree   Strongly Agree

I feel that I have a number of good qualities.

    Strongly Disagree   Disagree   Agree   Strongly Agree

I am able to do things as well as most other people.

    Strongly Disagree   Disagree   Agree   Strongly Agree

I feel I do not have much to be proud of.

    Strongly Disagree   Disagree   Agree   Strongly Agree

I certainly feel useless at times.

    Strongly Disagree   Disagree   Agree   Strongly Agree

I feel that I'm a person of worth, at least on an equal plane with others.

    Strongly Disagree   Disagree   Agree   Strongly Agree

I wish I could have more respect for myself.

    Strongly Disagree   Disagree   Agree   Strongly Agree

All in all, I am inclined to feel that I am a failure.

    Strongly Disagree   Disagree   Agree   Strongly Agree

I take a positive attitude toward myself.

    Strongly Disagree   Disagree   Agree   Strongly Agree

This section of questions is concerned with you and your family's experience with stigma as you were growing up. **Stigmatization refers to being judged or treated differently.** Please keep this definition in mind when answering the next list of questions.

Do you remember believing that your parent(s) were judged or treated differently because they had a child as a teenager?

                        Yes   No

On a scale from 0 to 100, how damaging would you say this experience was for your parents?

In the space below, please explain an example of a time your parent(s) were judged or treated differently because they had a child as a teenager.

How often do you remember your parent(s) feeling concerned about people treating them differently because they were a teenage parent?

Never   Rarely   Sometimes   Often   Always

How often do you remember your parent(s) feeling worried about people treating them differently because they were a teenage parent?

Never   Rarely   Sometimes   Often   Always

How often do you remember your parent(s) feeling scared about people treating them differently because they were a teenage parent?

Never   Rarely   Sometimes   Often   Always

How often do you remember your parent(s) feeling anxious about people treating them differently because they were a teenage parent?

Never   Rarely   Sometimes   Often   Always

How often do you remember your parent(s) feeling fearful about people treating them differently because they were a teenage parent?

Never   Rarely   Sometimes   Often   Always

The following questions are interested in understanding how any treatment your parents received influenced you. Please read them carefully and choose the option that best represents your experience as you grew up.

How often do you remember feeling concerned that the fact that your parent(s) were teenagers when you were born would influence how people viewed you?

Never   Rarely   Sometimes   Often   Always

How often do you remember feeling worried that the fact that your parent(s) were teenagers when you were born would influence how people viewed you?

Never   Rarely   Sometimes   Often   Always

How often do you remember feeling scared that the fact that your parent(s) were teenagers when you were born would influence how people viewed you?

Never   Rarely   Sometimes   Often   Always

How often do you remember feeling anxious about the fact that your parent(s) were teenagers when you were born would influence how people viewed you?

Never   Rarely   Sometimes   Often   Always

How often do you remember feeling fearful that the fact that your parent(s) were teenagers when you were born would influence how people viewed you?

Never   Rarely   Sometimes   Often   Always

This set of questions is interested in learning more about your personal experience with stigmatization. Remember, stigmatization refers to being judged or treated differently. Please answer them based on your experiences growing up.

Do you remember feeling judged or treated differently because your parents were teenagers when you were born?

Yes   No

On a scale from 0 to 100, how damaging would you say this experience was to you as a person.

In the following space, please describe an experience that represents a time you were judged or treated differently because your parents were teenagers when you were born.

How often do you remember feeling concerned about people treating you differently because your parents were teenagers when you were born?

Never   Rarely   Sometimes   Often   Always

How often do you remember feeling worried about people treating you differently because your parents were teenagers when you were born?

Never   Rarely   Sometimes   Often   Always

How often do you remember feeling scared about people treating you differently because your parents were teenagers when you were born?

Never   Rarely   Sometimes   Often   Always

How often do you remember feeling anxious about people treating you differently because your parents were teenagers when you were born?

Never   Rarely   Sometimes   Often   Always

How often do you remember feeling fearful about people treating you differently because your parents were teenagers when you were born?

Never   Rarely   Sometimes   Often   Always

Next you will be presented with five different behaviors you and your family may or may not have engaged in while you were growing up. For each behavior you will be provided with a definition of that behavior, followed by a hypothetical scenario that depicts a family engaging in that behavior. Please read each scenario carefully and consider whether you and your family engaged in the behavior as well.

Sometimes people feel the need to identify the nature of the relationship they have with other family members. An example of this is provided next.

Amy (aged 22) went out to run some errands and brought her younger brother, Matt, along. Her parents had her brother when she was 18, so he is much younger than her. While in line to pay for some groceries, a mother in line with her children mentioned how well-behaved Matt was and asked how she got so lucky. She was thankful for the comment, but worried the person assumed Matt was her son so she quickly said, "That's very kind of you! I can't take the credit though; he's just my brother. I'll have to ask our mom what her secret is!"

How frequently did you identify the relationship you had with family members, like Amy did with her brother?

Infrequently -- -- -- Frequently

Often -- -- -- Not Often

Rarely -- -- -- Regularly

Always -- -- -- Never

Sometimes people feel the need to explain their family relationships to others so they better understand those relationships. An example of this is given next.

Amy (age 22) went out with her mother to watch a local sporting event and two male patrons came up to them asking if they would like a drink. Amy and Laura politely declined, but the men stayed to chat. They mentioned that Amy and Laura looked alike and asked if they were sisters. The two ladies laughed and smiled, and let them know that they were, in fact, mother and daughter, not sisters. The men were shocked and said, "No way, you're joking right?" Laura smiled and said, "Yes, we are only 16 years apart, so we really are not that far apart in age."

How frequently did you explain the relationship you have with family members, like Amy did with her mother?

Infrequently -- -- -- Frequently

Often -- -- -- Not Often

Rarely -- -- -- Regularly

Always -- -- -- Never

Sometimes outsiders might not believe you when you explain how you are related to your family members. In these situations some people feel the need to help others realize that their family relationships are real and genuine. An example of this is given next.

The men from the bar were shocked that Laura could be Amy's mom and said, "Wow, that's crazy! I thought for sure you were sisters. I don't even believe you. There is no way that's true!" Amy responded by saying, "I know, I know. She actually is my mom though, I promise! I have the birth certificate to prove it!"

How frequently did you try to make others realize your family relationships were genuine, like Amy did with her mother?

Infrequently -- -- -- Frequently

Often -- -- -- Not Often

Rarely -- -- -- Regularly

Always -- -- -- Never

Sometimes other people might say something about your family that makes you upset. In those situations some people react by defending their family to others. An example of this is discussed next.

Amy (age 22) started a new job and started talking to a coworker about her plans for the weekend. She mentioned that it was her father's 39th birthday in a week so she was spending her weekend planning for the party. The coworker was surprised by the young age of her dad and said, "Wow that's really young. Is your life like those kids from the show on MTV, 16 and pregnant or whatever?" Amy was annoyed by the comparison and said, "It's actually nothing like that and honestly, my family is none of your business" then she walked away.

How frequently did you defend your family from others, like Amy did with her coworker?

Infrequently -- -- -- Frequently

Often -- -- -- Not Often

Rarely -- -- -- Regularly

Always -- -- -- Never

Some families tell stories about family members to one another as a way to help them understand their family relationships. An example of this is discussed next.

Amy (age 22) was cleaning out a closet in her parents' house one day and noticed a piece of art in the corner. She wasn't sure where it should go, so she grabbed the piece and asked her dad what he wants her to do with it. He said, "Oh, that's a painting I made back when I was in high school. Can you just put it on the table and I'll deal with it later?" Amy was surprised, she knew her dad was a decent artist, but had no idea he was that good, so she asked him about it. He told her a story about how he made the piece for a competition at school and was actually offered a scholarship to an art institute because of it. "But then we found out you were on the way, so I turned down the scholarship so I could get a job and start making money. It would have been fun, but I had responsibilities that were more important."

Infrequently -- -- -- Frequently

Often -- -- -- Not Often

Rarely -- -- -- Regularly

Always -- -- -- Never

This final section of the survey is interested in better understanding stories you might have been told from your family members throughout your life. Specifically, it is interested in learning more about stories you have heard regarding your conception, stories about experiences your family had while your mother was pregnant with you, and/or stories about your birth. Please take a moment to think about whether you have heard stories about any of these events.

Do you remember ever being told a story, or stories, about one or more of the events described here?

Yes   No

Please explain how you came to hear these stories (i.e., did you ask to hear them, did your family offer to tell them to you, and was it part of a tradition)

Please use the space provided to describe a story you were told by your family concerning either your birth, your family's experience while your mother was pregnant, or your conception.

Some of the stories people hear from family members are rather positive, and/ or happy, while others might be more negative and/or sad. Please indicate how you feel about the story you described previously.

Very Positive -- -- --- Very Negative

Unhappy -- -- -- Happy

Pleased -- -- -- Displeased

Dissatisfied -- -- -- Satisfied

Please use the space provided to describe the *most influential* story you were told by your family concerning either your birth, your family's experience while your mother was pregnant, or your conception.

Some of the stories people hear from family members are rather positive, and/or happy, while others might be more negative and/or sad. Please indicate how you feel about the story you described earlier.

Very Positive -- -- --- Very Negative

Unhappy -- -- -- Happy

Pleased -- -- -- Displeased

Dissatisfied -- -- -- Satisfied

Appendix D

Interview Schedule

1) What was it like for you growing up in a family with adolescent parents?
2) If you have one, tell me a story about a time you and/or your family members were treated differently because your parents were young.
3) Please explain how this experience influenced you.
4) Did your family ever tell you stories about your birth? If so, would you please tell me one that sticks out most to you?
5) Did your family ever tell you stories about your conception? If so, would you please tell me one that sticks out most to you?
6) Did your family ever tell you stories related to finding out your mother was pregnant with you? If so, would you please tell me the one that sticks out most to you?
7) How has your understanding of these stories changed over time, if at all?
8) Are there any other closing remarks you have concerning your family and your experience growing up with parents who were teenagers when you were born?

Index

About the Authors

Eryn N. Bostwick, PhD, is assistant professor at Texas Christian University and received her PhD in family communication from the University of Oklahoma (2018). She has been studying family communication since 2012, with a focus on the implications of negative communication processes within the family. Specifically, her published scholarship includes exploring family conflict, reasons for the decision to disclose or withhold secrets to one's parents, and adolescent parents' use of online support networks. Her work has been published in top journals, such as the *Journal of Social and Personal Relationships* and the *Journal of Family Communication*. Furthermore, she is a product of adolescent pregnancy, which has provided her with unique insight into the lives of her survey respondents/interviewees and allowed her to establish relationships that made the interviewees comfortable to talk about their experiences.

Amy Janan Johnson, PhD, is professor of communication and chair of the Department of Communication at the University of Oklahoma. She has been researching the influence of family communication on family relationships for over 20 years and has been published in top journals in the field including the *Journal of Family Communication* and *Journal of Social and Personal Relationships*, as well as well-known texts, such as *Contexts of the Dark Side of Communication*, edited by Eletra Gilchrest Petty and Shawn D. Long. Most recently Dr Johnson has been the editor of the *Western Journal of Communication*, one of the flagship publications of the Western States Communication Association.